Balancing Acts

Obligation, Liberation, And Contemporary Christian Conflicts

Henry G. Brinton

CSS Publishing Company, Inc., Lima, Ohio

BALANCING ACTS

Scripture quotations are from the *New Revised Standard Version of the Bible*, copyright 1989 by the Division of Christian Education of the National Council of the Churches of Christ in the USA. Used by permission.

Library of Congress Cataloging-in-Publication Data

Brinton, Henry G., 1960-
    Balancing acts : obligation, liberation, and contemporary Christian conflicts / Henry G. Brinton.
        p. cm.
    ISBN 0-7880-2386-1 (perfect bound : alk. paper)
    1. Church controversies. 2. Conservatism—Religious aspects—Christianity. 3. Liberalism—Religious aspects—Christianity. I. Title.

BV6529.B69 2006
250—dc22

2005029845

For more information about CSS Publishing Company resources, visit our website at www.csspub.com or email us at custserv@csspub.com or call (800) 241-4056.

Cover design by Barbara Spencer
ISBN 0-7880-2386-1

PRINTED IN U.S.A.

To my wife, Nancy,
and to my children,
Sarah and Sam

Table Of Contents

Acknowledgments

Since Christian beliefs and practices are always shaped by community, this book is the product of a number of congregations. My religious formation began in the church of my childhood, Christian Community Presbyterian Church in Bowie, Maryland, and has continued in the congregations I have served as a seminarian and a pastor: Sixth Presbyterian Church in Washington, D.C.; First Presbyterian Church in New Haven, Connecticut; First United Church of Christ in Milford, Connecticut; Calvary Presbyterian Church in Alexandria, Virginia; and Fairfax Presbyterian Church in Fairfax, Virginia. This book is also the product of the two academic communities which taught me to take the Bible seriously, if not always literally: Duke University and Yale Divinity School.

Friends and colleagues have offered me inspiration and encouragement. Dan Hans, a Presbyterian pastor in Milford, Connecticut, first opened my eyes to the covenant-exodus dichotomy. Bill Parent, Jay Tharp, and Jason DeParle have been friends for a quarter-century, and have been unfailing in their perceptive insights and moral support. My editors at the Outlook section of *The Washington Post*, where much of this material first appeared, have sharpened my writing and helped me to communicate these concerns to a wide community: Kate Boo, Jefferson Morley, Amy Waldman, Frances Sellers, Zofia Smardz, Elizabeth Ward, and Steve Luxenberg. I'm also grateful to Stan Purdum and Rebecca Brandt, editors at the CSS Publishing Company, for their interest in this book.

My family has always been a great support to my work as a pastor and a writer. I'm thankful to my parents, Henry and Mary Loraine Brinton, and to my brother, George, and his wife, Jodie, for their constant encouragement. Bill and Norma Freeborne, my in-laws, along with brother-in-law, Jay, have been a source of feedback and support. But most important of all are my children, Sarah and Sam, and my wife, Nancy. They are my obligation and my liberation.

Introduction

The pastor emeritus of Fairfax Presbyterian Church, the Virginia church I currently serve, was in Montgomery, Alabama, in March 1965 to hear the Reverend Martin Luther King, Jr.'s, speech at the end of his historic march from Selma. "We wanted to be there, and be part of the movement," Henry Baumann reflects. "Later, Fairfax church members took food to those attending the Poor People's March on Washington. There was a mood of support."

Growing up in the Presbyterian Church in the 1960s, I was shaped by stories like this. To the pastors and elders who were active in the church at that time, supporting King and other civil rights leaders seemed like no more than a faithful response to the call of the biblical prophets to work for social justice and to reshape the world. The focus was on liberation, as people of faith followed religious leaders on a journey to a new and better land.

But in mainline Protestant circles today, the atmosphere feels very different. Attention is given to obligation rather than to liberation, and passion is directed toward the preservation of traditional practices and beliefs. While liberal activists set the agenda in the 1960s, it is the conservative keepers of tradition that are dominating discussions today. "Conservatives are, by nature, supporters of the societal institutions and the standards of society," my parishioner, Jim Speer, points out. "The church institution is, historically, the societal moral anchor." Conservatives are drawn to the obligations of Christian life, the moral clarity of scripture, and the comfort of certain hymns and prayers.

Obligation and liberation — these are the two major spiritual themes that animate American religion, culture, and politics. As a writer and a pastor, I have discovered that Christians in this country tend to align themselves with one or the other. One group focuses on the obligations of religious life, and appreciates moral clarity — its scriptural foundation is covenant, an agreement defined by righteous living. The other group sees religion as a liberation movement and tends to stress God's love for the oppressed of the earth — it traces its spiritual roots to the exodus, when God brought the Israelites out of captivity in Egypt.

Biblically, I associate these opposing Christian camps with two dominant personalities from scripture: Abraham and Moses. Consciously or not, conservatives emulate Abraham, who made a covenant with God. Pat Robertson is a good example of Abrahamic obligation. Liberals, on the other hand, march behind Moses, who led his people out of captivity in Egypt in the exodus. Think of Jesse Jackson as a modern Moses.

Obligation versus liberation, clarity versus charity, covenant versus exodus — these are the opposing forces at the heart of our contemporary Christian conflicts. Both sides voice important themes in our religious tradition, and both have a contribution to make. But when one group surrenders, or drops out of the debate, the weight of mainstream opinion quickly shifts to the opposite side.

One reason the religious left is so weak today is that it hasn't had a charismatic leader since King. "In the '60s, white liberals in mainline Protestant churches were able to marshal a groundswell of activism to march in Selma with Dr. King," says Phil Beauchene, a member of my church. Forty years on, we still wrestle with racism, but "white liberals in today's churches who are concerned about racism have a hard sell getting their fellow parishioners excited about the methods and messages of Jesse Jackson and Al Sharpton," Beauchene asserts.

He's right. No one on today's scene can match King's powerful preaching or his ingenious blending of Gandhi's strategy of nonviolent resistance and Jesus' message of love for one's enemies. So the Christian majority turns its attention to other religious leaders, many of whom are simply repackaging traditional truths.

Is there a problem with this? Clearly, there is a place for time-honored certainties in our rapidly changing, high-tech world, but the obligations of religious life are only half the message. The message of liberation is equally urgent. After all, if traditional southern preachers had won the war of words in the early nineteenth century, we'd still have theological justification for slavery. If Christians had listened to white moderate pastors instead of black activist pastors in the '60s, they wouldn't have joined the Civil Rights Movement. And, if Protestant conservatives had dominated debate over the role of women in the church, there would be no female pastors in mainline congregations — some of the best preachers in the pulpit today.

One of these pastors, Susan Andrews at Bradley Hills Presbyterian Church in Bethesda, Maryland, has defined this theological tension as a balancing act between the truth of God and the grace of God. In a sermon to our National Capital Presbytery, she reminded us that Jesus handled this tension in surprising ways, sometimes breaking with traditional truths to lead people into God's grace. "Jesus healed on the Sabbath, he touched menstruating women, he put the needs of children before the needs of adults, he preferred the company of sinners over saints," she pointed out. "But we, in a changing, chaotic world, are often too scared to follow him."

The message of liberation is always a tough sell, because it requires a departure from tradition and a journey to a new place. That's hard for many Christians, especially those at the conservative, truth-of-God end of the spectrum, who don't necessarily want to follow Moses into the wilderness. Sometimes, however, that's exactly where church and society need to go, as difficult as the journey may be. On the other hand, liberal Christians sometimes find themselves lost in the wilderness, and they are challenged to recommit themselves to religious obligations in order to discover the direction God desires for them to travel. To be fully formed followers of Jesus Christ, we need to embrace obligation and liberation, clarity and charity, covenant and exodus, purity and diversity, exclusiveness and inclusiveness.

The opposing poles in our contemporary Christian conflicts — poles that are like oppositely charged terminals in the way they pull people of faith in opposite directions — can be summarized as follows:

11

Obligation	Liberation	
Covenant	Exodus	
Abraham	Moses	
Moral clarity	Christian charity	
Purity	Diversity	
Exclusiveness	Inclusiveness	
"Truth of God"	"Grace of God"	(Susan Andrews)
"Politics of purity"	"Politics of compassion"	(Marcus Borg)
"Hard America"	"Soft America"	(Michael Barone)

One note of caution: These opposing forces are much richer and deeper than the designations "conservative" and "liberal," and they will not always remain linked with a particular end of the political spectrum. Just as it would be absurd to label Abraham a Republican and Moses a Democrat, obligation and liberation cannot remain attached to the political right and left. In a time of war, for example, it is conservatives who tend to focus on the liberation of oppressed people, while it is liberals who lift up the obligation of nonviolence. The creative tension between obligation and liberation is valuable precisely because it does not remain trapped within our American political categories.

In the chapters that follow, you will see how this tension has played out in the trenches of congregational life — in particular, in the mainline churches I have served since the mid-1980s. Each chapter explores how obligation and liberation are present in our contemporary Christian conflicts, suggests how each can make creative contributions to the life of faith, and concludes with practical suggestions about how to manage or alleviate the tensions that inevitably arise between the two. The first chapter explores the delicate balancing acts performed by pastors and parishioners embracing competing sets of expectations, and the second takes a look at the impact of women on ministry. Chapters three and four reveal that Abraham and Moses have run repeatedly for President of the United States, and examine how obligation and liberation are expressed in church-state issues.

Returning to a focus on congregational life, the fifth chapter looks at the tension that has arisen between diversity and purity as immigrants have joined American congregations, and the sixth explores the balance between inclusiveness and exclusiveness that exists in every community of faith. Chapters seven through nine examine the interplay between hierarchies and democracies in the church today, between clarity and charity in Christian treatment of homosexuals, and between the exodus-orientation of young people and the covenant-focus of older men and women.

Chapter ten then digs into the dangers of individualistic religion, revealing how self-help spirituality weakens not only moral clarity, but also Christian charity. The final chapter looks at obligation and liberation in a time of war, and shows how these polarities do not always align themselves in a predictable way with conservative and liberal political positions. Whether you consider yourself to be an advocate of covenant or exodus, this report from the front lines should help you to understand more fully the conflicts that continue to challenge and divide the churches of the United States. It will also offer you some practical suggestions about how to manage these tensions in your own church and community.

It is certainly true that people of faith are feeling the strain of these conflicts in congregations across the country. More often than not, communities feel pulled apart by debates over moral clarity and Christian charity, purity and diversity, exclusiveness and inclusiveness — along with other manifestations of the obligation-liberation dichotomy. But, because Christians are uniquely positioned in our society as a community united by "one Lord, one faith, one baptism" (Ephesians 4:5), church remains the best place to wrestle with these issues and find some common ground in an increasingly fragmented world. Since both obligation and liberation are critical to our faith, we are challenged to keep the two in a state of truly creative tension.

In short, a balancing act.

Chapter One

Liberation And Obligation
In Congregational Life

They had been together six years, and their relationship was dying. Trust had broken down, communication was poor, and love had faded. As a friend and local clergyman, I had known them both for years and heard about their troubles: They were discovering that their expectations and values were very different, and they didn't see how they would be able to stay together.

This was no ordinary marriage. It was a relationship between a ministerial colleague of mine and a Presbyterian congregation. "A couple of the elders became absolutely hostile toward me in the course of the last year," the pastor told me, "misrepresenting me, distorting the truth." On the other hand, it was said that the pastor just didn't feel comfortable with many people in the church — this report came from a parishioner I had come to know and respect through a Christian education program. "And he didn't, at the end, like us very well." As I sat in the homes of these two neighbors and listened to the tale of their breakup, I understood why they had chosen to divorce.

Stories like this one are all too common today. Many relationships between pastors and parishes that begin with love and acceptance end in hostility and rejection, with the hopes for long-term unions of ten years or perhaps even forty suddenly dashed. While it is true that many ambitious pastors voluntarily jump to larger and larger churches throughout their careers, recent studies show that about one-fourth of all pastors have been forced out of at least one congregation, and many more choose to leave when they see the handwriting on the wall.

Conflicts of this sort are not limited to Presbyterians, the branch I grew up in and have served as a pastor since the late 1980s. Forced dissolutions appear to be on the rise among Roman Catholics, Southern Baptists, Lutherans, and Episcopalians. "Fights are dirtier, nastier, and more devastating than they used to be," said the Reverend Teri Thomas, general presbyter of my regional church body, National Capital Presbytery, in 1998. "In our more individualistic culture, we are now very willing to sacrifice the church for the sake of winning the battle."

Leadership magazine, a publication for the Christian clergy, conducted a random survey of approximately 600 U.S. pastors in 1996, and found that forced exits (defined as either termination or intense pressure to resign) are a chronic problem in the ministry. Twenty-three percent of current pastors have been forced out of churches at some point in their ministry. Some of the chief reasons for being forced out are conflicting visions of the church (46 percent); personality conflict with board members (38 percent); unrealistic expectations held by pastors (32 percent); personality conflicts with parishioners besides board members (22 percent); and theological differences (21 percent). A more recent study, part of the Pulpit & Pew research project at Duke Divinity School, was based on a 2002 survey of 963 ex-pastors. It revealed that the number one cause of congregational conflicts is disputes over pastoral leadership style, followed by finances and changes in worship style.

Although outsiders may see this as an internal church matter, and insiders may be too embarrassed to look at it squarely, the health of pastor-parish relationships is important to the community at large. With 44 percent of the U.S. population attending church in any given week according to a 1997 University of Michigan survey, pastor-parish relationships have a broad impact. Congregations are among the intermediate institutions — larger than a family but smaller than the national government — that sociologists and philosophers look to when they assess the health of a society. I know from personal experience that if clergy are working well with their congregations, leading them toward greater unity and community service, society benefits. One of the most successful programs at Calvary Presbyterian Church in Alexandria, Virginia, which I served as pastor from 1989 to 2000, was a tutoring program which not only helped unify our congregation but also benefited the children of our neighborhood. But when pastors and parishes fight, outreach programs suffer and the acrimony seeps out into the world.

What causes these destructive breakups? We've all read about extreme cases — of clergy manipulating or exploiting congregations by committing sexual or financial misconduct, but that certainly didn't happen with my colleague. More commonly, according to the Reverend John McDuffie, president of the Washington Episcopal Clergy Association, it boils down to questions of change: The clergy has a "vision of the parish growing in its mission and ministry," and of it "helping to stretch its boundaries to be more inclusive, welcoming new ways of carrying out organizational tasks, and encouraging a new corps of lay leaders to emerge." But these changes create conflict, pitting the expectations and values of the pastor against the expectations and values of the established lay leadership. It comes down to a battle between liberation and obligation.

I know how hard it is both to be faithful to a congregation's traditions (obligations) and to bring to it new challenges (liberation). I well remember my grueling interview with a dozen members of Calvary's pastor-nominating committee when I was a candidate for the position in 1988. For three hours, questions were fired at me by parishioners who were young, old, male, female, newcomers, longtime members, and believers from across the theological spectrum. I was convinced as I struggled through that I was angering as many people as I was pleasing. Fortunately, the committee realized that no candidate would be able to make every church member happy. They hired me and, sure enough, I didn't make everyone happy, especially with the incorporation of large numbers of young African immigrants into our congregation, bringing racial, cultural, and generational changes that no one (including myself) fully anticipated.

But the clash of expectations at my colleague's church was at first far more difficult to identify and ultimately more damaging. He — and some members — wanted the congregation to grow and change, to become more focused on outreach programs, following the liberation emphasis of the biblical exodus. But, other parishioners expected the minister to know the membership, to visit people in homes and meetings, and to concentrate on sermon preparation, focusing on a set of obligations that align most closely with traditional covenant-keeping. Each set of goals was worthwhile, but no Christian leader short of Christ could hope to attain them all. (As a Roman Catholic priest once said to me, Jesus was perfect, and they nailed him to a cross!) The Pulpit & Pew research project at Duke revealed that problems often arise for "innovative young pastors faced with traditional don't-change-anything older adults." Young pastors who want to help their congregations to grow and change (liberation!) often butt heads with older adults who want their ministers to meet their personal needs (obligation!).

These tensions associated with attracting new members to churches are evident throughout the Washington area, as neighborhoods become more socially, culturally, and racially diverse. Conflicting values are a further source of difficulty, whether the battle lines are drawn between purity and diversity, or between moral clarity and Christian charity. When I was doing a research project on the incorporation of African immigrants into American churches in 1996, looking for ways to build unity in my own increasingly multicultural congregation, I met the Reverend Marcia Cox. She served a Lutheran church in southern Maryland from 1989 to 1996, and during her tenure, attendance increased from 65 to 200 each Sunday. This success was marred, however, by what Marcia calls "a downright power struggle" between herself and fifteen families.

At issue were a number of controversial decisions, including her denial of a church member's request to sing a Bette Midler tune at Christmas Eve services. The woman wanted to sing "From A Distance" in front of her family, and Marcia objected. In this case, the pastor was the purist — she felt that the lyrics "God is watching us from a distance" were theologically incompatible with the message that God had entered human life in the Christ-child. The conflict made a group of members leave, prompting a temporary financial crisis (power was cut and a photocopier repossessed). Although the request to sing a particular song — and the pastor's response to it — might seem insignificant at first, it illustrates important differences in values.

According to Marcia, ministers leave their training at seminaries with a strong grounding in the Bible and theology, and enter parishes believing that they are bringing the right answers. "This adds to our inflexibility," she admitted, and I would have to agree, remembering an argument I had with an elder in a previous church about the "correct" way to structure a service. Congregations, on the other hand, value local tradition and are convinced that their experience gives them insight into how things ought to be done. They can be just as inflexible as pastors. My friend, Kent Winters-Hazelton, an interim-ministry specialist, tells me that an experienced pastor once advised him, "If you want to be effective in your ministry, you have to allow [parishioners] to be who they are." Pastors have to pick their purity battles carefully, and do what they can to honor the diverse perspectives that will inevitably be found among their church members.

I often grapple with knowing where to draw the line between allowing people "to be who they are" and preserving biblical and theological values. I felt comfortable with my decision, prior to an interfaith wedding, to deny a Jewish bride's request to remove all the crosses from the church so as not to offend her family. They ended up being married elsewhere. But, I wonder if I gave in too quickly to congregational pressure to restore the baptismal font to the front of the church, where people could watch the sacrament more easily. (I felt it belonged at the door of the sanctuary, to preserve the symbolic link between baptism and entry into the Christian community.) Each week, I struggle with choosing hymns that people love to sing versus those that have the most timely message; whether to preach a message of comfort or one of challenge; how to speak the truth to hundreds of distinct, diverse individuals. As the Reverend Stephen Welch, executive director of the Mount Vernon Baptist Association, says, "A body of people with conflicted values will be limited. Leaders with different values than those they serve will be frustrated."

Of course, some conflict is inevitable in a church that is growing and engaged in Christian ministry. I'd like to think we can all learn from it, even profit from it. In preparation, seminaries should link classes on Bible and theology with courses on understanding church family systems, crossing cultural boundaries, and leading congregations through organizational change. (At least half the ex-pastors in the Pulpit & Pew study have asserted that seminary training is "not practical and realistic enough" in its preparation of people for parish ministry.) In addition, churches should institute "pastor-parish relationship committees" that do not have power to hire and fire, but oversee the pastoral role. A committee like this would help "bring conflict to the surface and get it worked out," suggested my clergy colleague as he was leaving his church. Such a committee could look at the tensions that are bound to arise between pastors and parishioners over issues of liberation and obligation, diversity and purity, Christian charity and moral clarity.

A few years ago at Calvary, I entered a protracted struggle with a number of older members when I expressed excitement about the arrival of large numbers of newcomers into our church. It turned into a battle between the opposing virtues of diversity and purity, with some of us feeling very positive about our newfound racial-ethnic diversity and many other members experiencing a tremendous sense of loss. The church that had felt so pure and comfortable to them and their families was rapidly changing into something that might no longer feel like their spiritual home.

My hunch was that developing personal relationships would be the secret to navigating this difficult passage: relationships between pastor and parishioner, and between longtime members and newcomers. I hoped that over time some friendships would begin as people of different ages and cultures rubbed elbows during worship, coffee hours, committee meetings, and workdays. And, in fact, many important bonds did develop, and a number of people discovered that Calvary could be a home to a wide variety of people, old and new. One day, I was deeply touched as I saw one of our elders, a retiree named Alvin Anderson, walk forward at a meeting of National Capital Presbytery and publicly embrace Stephen Nkansah, a Ghanaian parishioner who had become a candidate for ordained ministry.

I learned at Calvary that I would still have conflicts with members who did not share my vision, but this did not mean that I could not care for them — and they for me. Maybe that is what pastor-parish marriages are really all about: Developing open and honest relationships across the obligation-liberation divide, and discussing the differences that challenge, but also enliven, the life of the Christian community. In fact, I have come to see that one challenge for clergy is to embrace the tension that is bound to exist in pastor-parish relationships — to embrace it as one of the most important balancing acts that any pastor is called to perform. Since churches should hang on to both obligation and liberation, weighing one and then the other in discussion and debate, a pastor's inability to move in perfect sync with church members is not necessarily a bad thing.

It is certainly no surprise that clergy are often out of step with their people. Ron Sellers, the president of Ellison Research, a national Christian marketing research company based in Phoenix, tells me that "clergy in mainline churches tend to be more liberal theologically and politically than the people in their pews." Mainline clergy are more liberation oriented than their people, and I know this — I've long been aware that I am more progressive than my parishioners in many areas, pushing them, for example, to be more accepting of diversity in the life of the church.

But my evangelical colleagues are equally out-of-line. According to Sellers, most evangelical pastors are more conservative than the people they are leading, and they have a focus on purity that puts them closer to the obligation end of the spectrum. Sellers tells me that the typical evangelical church theology calls for a conservative lifestyle, but studies show that there is a surprising lack of lifestyle differences between born-again Christians and the general population. In fact, there are no differences at all in the divorce rate, the likelihood of seeing an R-rated movie, or the likelihood of watching MTV. Across the United States, it seems that the influence of religion on lifestyle, worldview, and politics is really very small, whether you are a liberal or a conservative.

So a gap exists between pastors and parishioners, on the left and on the right. On many political and sociological issues, there is going to be a disconnect between ministers and the congregations they serve, and this sounds like a difficult — and perhaps even dangerous — situation. But, the more I ponder this state of affairs, the more I realize that it does not have to be a crippling problem. Instead, it can be a truly creative tension.

After all, we preachers are supposed to stand apart from our people and challenge them morally and spiritually. Liberal clergy are invited to play the role of the prophet Moses, challenging their people to work for the liberation of the oppressed and to venture toward a promised land. Conservative pastors can imitate the patriarch Abraham as they focus on religious obligations and preserve the time-honored covenant with God. Both liberals and conservatives have important roles to play in the life of faith, because Christianity simultaneously looks ahead to a promised land and back to a covenant, even as it honors both liberation and obligation.

So, if pastors feel a gap with their people, they should not despair — a difference in perspective does not mean that the pastor-parish match has not been made in heaven. The failure to be in sync with church members is actually part of the vitality of religious life, because leadership could not be exercised if pastors and parishioners were in step on every issue. Instead, churches should make the effort to establish "pastor-parish relationship committees" to oversee the pastoral role and discuss the conflicts that are bound to exist in a lively community of faith over purity and diversity, clarity and charity, covenant and exodus. Real unity can be experienced as pastors and parishioners work together in local mission projects that meet the needs of the community, as the Eagle's Wings Tutoring Program has done in Alexandria, Virginia. There is no reason that personal relationships cannot be developed across the boundaries that so often divide us, especially if pastors work to bring people together during worship, coffee hours, committee meetings, and church workdays.

As pastors and parishioners learn to live with the tensions that are inherent in their relationships, they'll discover that a healthy church needs the contributions of those who are committed to obligation as well as the contributions of those who have a passion for liberation. After all, obligation-keeping can become an inward-looking, self-centered activity unless pastors challenge people to look outward and join the exodus; in similar fashion, liberation-seeking can become an experience of wandering in the wilderness unless ministers challenge people to look inward and remember the covenant. Every pastor has a role to play in the maintenance of this creative tension, as they challenge people to embrace their deepest commitments while also moving ever closer to a new and better land.

Chapter Two

When The Minister Is A Mother

On a break from seminary in 1984, I earned a few bucks by preaching a sermon at my home church in Bowie, Maryland, which at the time was looking for a new pastor. With the insolence of youth, I called on the congregation to have "the nerve and the faith" to consider "installing a woman as the pastor of this church." "I can tell you," I went on, "coming from a divinity school which is a full fifty percent women, that the future of the Protestant Church is going to be shaped in large part by the decisions of female leaders."

The members of the congregation were shocked — or so I was later told. Most had no idea that women were flocking to seminary in such large numbers. However, if I were to preach that same sermon today, I suspect my words would be greeted by yawns. These days, people know that the minister can be a mother.

Women are taking over leading roles in at least eighty denominations (although they are barred from ordination by about the same number) — and the change has been swift. As author Cullen Murphy pointed out in his book, *The Word According to Eve*, between 1992 and 1996 the number of women enrolled in master's programs in divinity grew by fifteen percent, while the percentage of men in such programs declined. The feminization of divinity school is leading to a feminization of the pulpit, and we may see the day when ministry is a female-dominated profession.

All across the country, Christians are discovering that the next minister of their local church won't necessarily be an unmarried young man fresh out of college and seminary. There's a good chance this "man of the cloth" will be a divorced, middle-aged woman entering the ministry as a second career, with teenaged kids in tow, and she'll bring to her work a markedly less formal, more therapeutic style. Ordained ministry has now been liberated from centuries of male domination, but the fact of the matter is that some parishioners aren't quite ready for this change. They are looking for a male Abraham in the pulpit, and what they get is a female Moses.

Yes, it's true that some Protestant denominations still discourage women from pursuing ministry. And yes, the Roman Catholic Church continues to bar women from the priesthood. Yet in spite of these obstacles, women of all denominations are flocking to seminary. In National Capital Presbytery, where I served as the co-chair of the committee on preparation for ministry in the early 1990s, we had forty women and 35 men preparing for service to the Presbyterian Church (USA). Similarly, during those years I learned that Wesley Theological Seminary in Washington, D.C., was 56 percent female, and Christian Theological Seminary in Indianapolis stood at 52 percent. The student body of my alma mater, Yale Divinity School, was 47 percent women, and the average age was 34. In this traditionally Protestant school, interestingly, the second largest denominational group was Roman Catholic, and among these Catholics the majority were women.

Is this good news? Yes and no. Like teaching and nursing, ministry has now become a high-stress, low-status profession, and the best students coming out of college often choose other professions with higher status and greater financial rewards. Into the vacuum have stepped a group of older women who bring special strengths to ministry, including caring and compassion. Many emphasize pastoral counseling, as opposed to church administration, and bring an interest in the more nurturing aspects of human life.

These women clearly fit the liberation mold, with their passion for Christian charity, caring, and compassion. One of them, the Reverend Barbara Sloop, was in her forties when she graduated from Louisville Seminary and accepted a call to be an associate pastor at Second Presbyterian Church in Indianapolis, the largest Presbyterian church in Indiana. A retired captain in the U.S. Public Health Service, she worked twenty years as a physical therapist, administrator, and educator, and her sense of vocation came from working with people suffering from leprosy and then AIDS, alongside Surgeon General C. Everett Koop. "I began to see," she told me in 1994, "that for some people, healing could come only through a relationship with God, and a life beyond this one."

A story like this one makes me glad that ministry has been liberated from the control of wet-behind-the-ears young men. On a personal level, an experienced caregiver such as Barbara Sloop is bound to have more empathy for the problems and needs of her parishioners than a 25-year-old man right out of seminary, and the expertise and perspective of a medical career is bound to be an asset to parish ministry. In the sociopolitical sphere, I agree with Sloop that it is important that "women and people of color are making the ministry more representative of the world."

Still, an all-rose-colored view of older women in ministry is probably too simplistic. When I was a seminarian at Yale in the '80s, we had a cruel nickname for older students: "the mid-life crisis crowd." We saw that many people were coming to seminary after unsatisfying careers, and some had been broken by divorce or addictions. For them, divinity school was not simply an academic institution — it was a place to search for healing and personal fulfillment. Licensed psychologist and ordained Lutheran minister, L. Guy Mehl, who spent more than two decades working with ministerial candidates at the Lancaster Career Development Center in Pennsylvania, observed that many seminarians in the early 1990s were "coming out of traumatic, change-filled and painful backgrounds." Many grew up in broken homes, many had been sexually abused, many had either been addicted or had come from families in which addiction was present, and many had been divorced. A good number of these students were mid-life women.

With personal histories of rescuing dysfunctional family members, such candidates "will be natural rescuers in church settings," Mehl said. What they will not be, he feared, were vigorous, assertive church leaders. They will naturally be more comfortable in speaking a word of liberation from pain and suffering than in confronting hard questions of obligation and proclaiming difficult truths. Nonetheless, Mehl was hopeful about this new generation of clergy. These "caregivers and nurturers," he said, "may be what our society needs at this time in its history."

27

Sure, society may need these liberation leaders, but does it want them? At seminaries around the country, many well-qualified older women are having trouble finding what's known in this business as "a call." In the Presbyterian system, it is not enough to be called by God — you also have to be called by a church or some other place of ministry. Through my work with the committee on preparation for ministry, I saw many gifted women complete seminary, pass their ordination exams and then wait months, or even years, before receiving a call. Some candidates, sadly, may never receive a call and be ordained.

Why such trouble even for women especially gifted at pastoral care, and committed to helping people? My own experience with female candidates is that they can express their faith with great sincerity, intelligence, and creativity. Where they sometimes run into trouble is in communicating that faith to church members who are accustomed to very traditional language and images. While they have Moses' gift of charity, they fail to bring Abraham's gift of clarity into their statements to the Christian community.

"It's not enough to say what you believe," I told one candidate when I was on the committee on preparation for ministry. "You've also got to build a bridge between yourself and the church." This is inevitably discouraging to a woman who has worked long and hard to create a very personal statement of faith. It leaves her wondering if she'd be better off standing before the committee and reciting the traditional Apostles' Creed.

Another reason for the reluctance to embrace women must be summed up as a failure of institutional imagination. Many church-people are unaccustomed to having women serve as authority fig-ures — they have not completely embraced the liberation of the pastoral role from male domination. Sam Alexander, a second-ca-reer seminarian at Richmond's Union Theological Seminary, was frustrated at watching several qualified female classmates sweat out a placement while he was in school. He said to me, "Search committees don't have an 'image' of how a woman would look in the pastorate." Churches still tend to want a man under age forty, married to a nonworking woman who volunteers on church com-mittees — a profile that might sound horribly out-of-date, but in fact comes from a 2003 study by sociologist Adair Lummis, published as part of the Pulpit & Pew project at Duke Divinity School.

Other denominations, such as the Methodists, give women a better chance through a system that simply assigns seminary graduates to congregations. Even then, there is no guarantee that church members will truly accept a person who does not fit their vision of a manly pastor. In Prince George's County, Maryland, one Methodist Church watched attendance drop through the pastorates of two able women. As soon as a male pastor was assigned to the church, participation shot up.

Clearly, the issue of women in ministry does more than raise questions about equal-opportunity employment — it also has an impact on the life and character of the entire church. Much as I support the arrival of women in lay and ordained leadership positions, I can't help having some concerns about this male-to-female transition as I see it playing out around me. I wonder: Does the presence of women in leadership roles cause men — both parishioners and prospective clergy — to shy away from the church, or encourage them to abdicate their religious obligations? And what effect does this change have on those members — often female — who have long considered pastors to be paternal figures? The conventional wisdom among ministers is that most of the resistance to female pastors comes from women in the pews. For older women, especially widows, the pastor is a very important *man* in their life.

Any number of churchgoers would agree with Nana Adu-Gyamfi, one of my male elders at Calvary Presbyterian Church, who told me, "A woman — my sister — brought me to God. Why should it bother me if a woman is a pastor?" But I know, anecdotally, that there is discomfort, and that it generally goes unspoken. There are people who simply don't feel at ease with a female pastor, any more than some people do with male nurses in a hospital.

A seminary classmate and colleague, Leah Schafer, associate pastor of St. Mark's Lutheran Church in Springfield, Virginia, reports that she is very well accepted at the moment. But she says that one couple in her previous congregation in D.C. "refused to let me even visit them because they were against women in the ministry. ... I have found that church individuals who are not pillars or

29

leaders are very accepting of me until a 'public' event, such as a baptism, marriage, or funeral happens. Then — all things being equal — they will go with a male."

There's more to this shift than an influx of women like Leah in leadership positions. Feminist theology is jumping off the bookshelves, women are packing programs on "soul work," and lay and ordained female leaders are expressing some of the freshest and liveliest ideas about the life of faith. "I think women are seekers looking for connections and anchors to make sense of all that happens in life," Jackie McDaniel, a Fairfax County (Virginia) school administrator and Presbyterian elder, told me. She suspects that the mystery of faith may be more palatable to women than to men.

My colleague Margee Iddings, a minister who was moderator of meetings at National Capital Presbytery when I came to Calvary in 1989, echoes Jackie's thoughts. Now the director of a retreat center called "Rising Phoenix," which attracts a clientele that is eighty percent female, she observes that women have traditionally been encouraged to pay attention to their "inner selves." Margee, Jackie, and female leaders such as Leah, bring a perspective that is much more experiential, communal, and comfortable with mystery than the theoretical, individualistic, and rational approach so often favored by men. Surveys within the Presbyterian Church (USA) reveal that 44 percent of female pastors label themselves as theologically liberal, compared to just 23 percent of male pastors. At the other end of the spectrum, only thirteen percent of female pastors describe themselves as theologically conservative — the label chosen by 33 percent of male pastors.

So far, there are few signs that this new focus is causing men to flee to the nearest exit. But I have been told by several researchers that some African-American churches have traditionally reserved the top lay and clergy roles for men, not only for theological but also for practical reasons. In some congregations, I've learned, there is fear that if these roles are filled by women, then men will disappear.

What's more, there is clearly a market for churches with Abraham-style, all-male leadership. The Presbyterian Church in America, a denomination formed a quarter-century ago in a split with mainline Presbyterians such as myself, bans the ordination of women to any office but allows churches to appoint women to assist male deacons. The denomination boasts a 2.4 percent annual growth rate, and is one of the fastest-growing religious groups in the country. In contrast, most female-friendly mainline denominations have experienced a dramatic decline in church membership since the 1960s.

The popularity of the Promise Keepers movement also suggests that men may be looking for a masculine format for religious practice. Its leaders speak a language of manly challenges — of struggle, commitment, and spiritual warfare — a kind of "Onward, Christian Soldiers" battle cry for a new age. Of course, Promise Keepers is not for everyone, and few men in my church have shown any interest in this style of ministry. But a number of men have told me that they would rather come to a men's group to "drive nails" than to "discuss issues."

So, what can be done to keep men connected to church? In the fall of 2004, I was part of a group of thirteen mid-life men who traveled to Honduras to experience another culture, help build a church camp for children, develop community among ourselves, and perhaps, even, experience some personal transformation. We started work as early as 6:30 in the morning, and often labored until 6:00 at night, digging postholes, pouring concrete, carrying cinderblocks, lifting steel beams. Then we would return to our hotel for clean-up, happy hour, and dinner, followed by a time of Bible study and reflection. We were inspired and energized by the work we were doing, and came out of the week feeling close to God and to each other, already talking about another mission trip.

This experience worked for the men of the church because it was far from home (away from office demands, telephones, and email), physically challenging, and task-oriented. They returned home with a desire to recruit additional men for future trips, and some talked of developing a companion experience for entire families, so that wives and children could share the experience.

The success of this mission trip was due, I believe, to the fact that it was an experience that appealed to male sensibilities. It was an adventure that pulled men away from their daily lives for a week

31

of hard work, community-building, and spiritual growth, and then challenged them to re-engage with the church at a deeper level. I am convinced that it would be worthwhile for any congregation concerned about male involvement to organize such a mission trip for the men of the church, and to consider leaving the country in order to disconnect participants from their cell phones and computers. A number of the men admitted to me that the week would not have been as valuable to them if they had remained closer to home, in touch with their families and coworkers.

This talk of adventurous all-male mission trips may suggest more of a dichotomy than typically exists between men's and women's religious styles. But the ongoing engagement of men in the church is a serious concern, and we need to be ready to address these as well as more subtle questions that come with the increased feminization of the church. A female candidate for ordination has told me that she is concerned that ministerial salaries will drop as women flood the field. And an elder at Calvary Presbyterian, Lisa Simpson, also thinks that the inclusive language movement — which represents another form of feminization in the church by making the language of hymns and scripture gender-neutral — has gone too far, that it has the potential to alienate both men and women who believe that the preservation of tradition is important. Here again is a desire for obligation over liberation.

This is not to say that women should have to defend their leadership roles to me or anyone else. Far from it. Women are (and always have been) at the core of the church, and I am grateful for the ministry being performed by women such as Carrie Yearick, my associate pastor at Fairfax Presbyterian Church in Fairfax, Virginia, where I have served as senior pastor since 2001. The membership of this congregation is 52 percent female — a proportion typical of my denomination (my previous congregation was even higher, 61 percent). Women are clearly the majority party in Christianity, and I'm told by Cynthia Woolever of the Presbyterian Church's office of research services that in our denomination they are better represented than men at church programs and events, and that more women than men pray and read the Bible every day.

This fits my experience at Calvary and Fairfax, where women play essential roles at every level of church life, and I suspect it fits the experience of religious leaders through the ages. According to the Bible, Jesus welcomed women to positions of prominence in his ministry and appeared first to Mary Magdalene after his resurrection on Easter morning. Sixteen of the forty people that the Apostle Paul mentions in his epistles are women. New Testament scholar Helmut Koester, who recently retired from Harvard Divinity School, points out that chapter 16 of Romans (the earliest known letter of recommendation for a Christian minister) is written for a woman, Phoebe, who was a deacon or minister of the church at Cenchreae. I've been asked to recommend women for ministerial positions — and will continue to do so without reservation. And, when I was chairman of the committee on preparation for ministry, I couldn't help but be struck by the fact that most of our top candidates were women.

We should continue to embrace this change. But even as we do so, we need to recognize that we do ourselves no favors if we plow ahead without thoughts about its broader impact. In the end, the feminization of the church can't help but be a good thing if it balances and corrects the predominantly masculine qualities that have marked Christian leadership for the last two millennia. We definitely need female leaders who can provide ministry that is therapeutic and relational, working alongside men who have a more confrontational and authoritative style. At the same time, congregations should provide men with programs such as adventurous, action-oriented mission trips, to offer a counterweight to the female-friendly discussion groups and spiritual-growth experiences that have been growing in recent years.

Since "there is no longer male and female," according to the Apostle Paul, but rather unity in Christ (Galatians 3:28), the church is at its best when all kinds of persons learn, live, and serve faithfully together. I believe that as long as leaders provide opportunities that are in tune with both masculine and feminine sensibilities, it should not matter whether they are men or women. Pastors are effective not because of gender, but because they balance clarity and charity as they connect their people with God.

Chapter Three

Abraham And Moses
Run For President

George W. Bush is Abraham. Bill Clinton is Moses. Peel back the party affiliations, and you discover that these two presidents of the United States have strong ties to a patriarch and a prophet. Clinton has a faith that focuses on liberation, while Bush tends to stress religious obligation. In their words and deeds on the campaign trail and in the White House, they reveal allegiance to two distinctive models of religious leadership that have roots in the deepest strata of Hebrew history.

But perhaps it is premature to jump immediately to the conclusion that Bush and Clinton are *religious* leaders, even though both men speak openly and often about their Christian faith. Better to go back a few years, to an earlier election cycle in which two ordained ministers made a run for the White House. The year was 1988, and Jesse Jackson and Pat Robertson were racing full speed along the presidential campaign trail. Both were Baptists, and while they might have shared some foundational Christian beliefs, their political views were wildly divergent.

Marion "Pat" Robertson was a conservative who was expected to continue the "Reagan Revolution" with strong views on issues such as abortion, school prayer, and pornography. He yielded his Southern Baptist ministry credentials in an effort to separate his religious vocation from his candidacy, but some questioned his dedication to the separation of church and state. While a minister, Robertson said he believed that only devout Christians and Jews were qualified to govern.

Such stands led some evangelical Christians to call Robertson "God's candidate for the presidency of the United States." But it was not only evangelicals that were lining up behind him: The Robertson campaign was staffed by Christians of all kinds, including Roman Catholics and mainstream Protestants. His message seemed to resonate with people who felt afflicted by "secular humanism" and were anxious for a national move toward Judeo-Christian values.

On the other hand, Jesse Jackson was a liberal who was highly critical of the Reagan administration. His support seemed to be coming from groups which felt powerless at the time, both his multiracial Rainbow Coalition that emerged during the 1984 campaign, and groups of farmers, Vietnam veterans, and blue-collar workers. Unlike Robertson, Jackson held on to his Baptist ministry credentials and managed to avoid becoming embroiled in the church-state debate. Perhaps his racial-ethnic background provided him with some protection, since in the African-American community it is not uncommon for ministers to be leaders in both religious and political spheres.

Jackson believed that he was set aside by God for a purpose, according to an article by Gail Sheehy in the January 1988 *Vanity Fair*, and he had a dream while in high school in which he was leading his people across a river. Apparently, this revealed to him that he was a born leader, one who could go on to assist Martin Luther King, Jr., confront Mikhail Gorbachev on the question of Soviet Jewry, challenge Daniel Ortega to reopen the Nicaraguan press, and, of course, run for president of the United States. "From the outhouse to the statehouse to the courthouse to the White House," was his vision, as preached to the congregation of New Bethel Baptist Church in Detroit in the summer of 1987. Jesse Jackson was a man who dreamed of leading his people, and not just the Rainbow Coalition but all the people of the United States.

Pat Robertson and Jesse Jackson: Two committed Christians with wildly different political visions. One is a conservative, one is a liberal ... one is devoted to traditional societal structures, one is devoted to the underclass ... one believes that only the devout should govern, the other believes that he has been called to lead his people across the river. All of which raises the question: Are they merely different kinds of politicians, or are they actually different kinds of Christians?

The distinctions between Pat Robertson and Jesse Jackson go beneath their political positions to their basic religious orientations. Put quite simply, one focuses on covenant, while the other orients himself toward exodus. Pat Robertson has a view of life and faith that centers on an agreement with God, a covenant, while Jesse Jackson bases his convictions on God's liberating work, seen most clearly in the exodus. Believers such as Robertson tend to focus on the obligations of religious life, and they appreciate moral clarity, while Christians such as Jackson see religion as a liberation movement and tend to stress God's love for the oppressed of the earth.

Of course, neither of these orientations is uniquely Christian. Both are based in the Hebrew Scriptures and are central to Jewish thought as well. In the book of Genesis, God makes a covenant with Abraham, the great patriarch of the Israelites. God says, "I am God Almighty; walk before me, and be blameless. And I will make my covenant between me and you, and will make you exceedingly numerous" (Genesis 17:1-2). God makes a deal with Abraham: He says "walk before me, and be blameless," and I will do wonderful things for you. In exchange for Abraham's devotion, God promises to multiply Abraham, to make him exceedingly fruitful, to establish him as the father of a multitude of nations, with kings and a land that his family could call its own.

This is covenant in its classic sense: A term of relationship between a superior and an inferior party, with the superior party — in this case God — establishing the bond and setting the terms. Throughout the Hebrew Scriptures, God renews this covenant with the people of Israel over and over, and the deal is always basically the same: You shall be my people and I will be your God.

The other focal point presented in the Bible is the exodus, the mighty act in which God liberates his people from slavery in Egypt. Knowing that the Hebrews have suffered, God comes down "to deliver them from the Egyptians, and to bring them up out of that land to a good and broad land, a land flowing with milk and honey" (Exodus 3:8). Moses is appointed to lead God's people out, and he does so, through the Red Sea and on toward the promised land. Throughout Jewish and Christian history, this event has been considered crucial to the life of faith, for it demonstrates

God's solidarity with the oppressed, and his desire to liberate people from physical and spiritual bondage.

Clearly, Pat Robertson is a kind of Abraham, in covenantal relationship with God and hoping to govern along with other people of the covenant — devout Christians and Jews. Jesse Jackson sees himself as a Moses, repeating the exodus as he leads his followers over the river and into the promised land. It is their orientation to one or the other of these foci, covenant or exodus, that governs their religious attitudes, and to some extent, their politics. It is not too much of a stretch to say that in 1988, Abraham and Moses ran for president.

Of course, Pat Robertson and Jesse Jackson are not the only politicians to embrace these orientations. In each election cycle, conservatives emulate the covenant-making character of Abraham, as they focus on the obligations of religious life and show an appreciation for moral clarity. Liberals continue to march behind Moses, as they embrace religion as a liberation movement and stress God's love for the oppressed of the earth. Obligation versus liberation, and clarity versus charity — these distinctive approaches continue to define the theological battle lines in church and society today.

Consider the positions of Bill Clinton, the Moses character of the 1990s. As president, he met regularly with ministers, claimed a relationship with Christ, and not only read the scriptures but quoted them from memory. In November 1995, he wept when Bishop Nathaniel Linsey of the Christian Methodist Episcopal Church and fourteen other clergy laid hands on him and asked God to "make the president strong for the task" of protecting society's most vulnerable. But in conservative circles there was always a great deal of consternation about Clinton's Christianity — especially his Baptist affiliation. The Southern Baptist Convention rejected Clinton's policies on moral issues, and passed a resolution that said "we separate ourselves" from the president's "acts and positions" supporting abortion rights, abortion funding, homosexuals in the military, and homosexual rights.

Conservatives wanted the president to provide moral clarity, but Clinton focused instead on Christian charity — using his office to help persons in need. Seminary professor, Wayne Ward, a former pastor to Clinton, said to *Christian American* magazine in March 1993, "Despite differences of opinion people may have with Bill, he is a disciple of Jesus Christ and sees the political profession as a way to fulfill his strong calling from God to help people." His policies were oriented more toward liberation than toward obligation, motivating him to work to protect freedoms such as gay rights and abortion rights. He would fall under the "Soft America" category defined by political analyst Michael Barone in his book, *Hard America, Soft America* — "Soft America" being a movement marked by progressive values, filled with government regulation and social safety nets.

In a sermon delivered on November 22, 1992, Jesse Jackson hailed Clinton's election as "the dawn of a new day," and announced that "God has raised up a leader from amongst the common people." Referring to the Ten Commandments, Jackson said that God gave Moses a "ten-point urban policy plan," and suggested that such ethical principles should guide ordinary Americans as they seek to fulfill their part of the Clinton agenda. For some, Bill Clinton served as a kind of Moses, a leader raised up by God to liberate the oppressed and create a better society. "Political involvement dictated by faith is not the exclusive province of the right wing," said Clinton at a Sunday service at New York's Riverside Church during the 2004 presidential campaign. The September 4, 2004, *Washington Post* reported that Riverside became the mother ship of "Mobilization 2004" and "Let Justice Roll," nationwide efforts to place "prophetic justice principles" in front of voters and candidates.

Replacing Clinton was George W. Bush, an Abraham for the new millennium. From the very start, he was pro-life and pro-traditional-family, and brought a focus on moral clarity that his predecessor could never provide (especially in light of the Monica Lewinsky scandal). "I rely upon my faith as an anchor, as a home, as a spiritual home that is very comforting," Bush told Crosswalk.com during the 2000 campaign. "I find great comfort in the Bible and in prayer." This attitude of intense devotion began for Bush in 1986, around his fortieth birthday, when he quit drinking and entered into a deeper relationship with God. Although he never went into a substance abuse program such as Alcoholics Anonymous, he indicated to *The Washington Post* in July 1999 that he was guided by the broader AA philosophy of placing one's faith in God. "If you change your heart, you can change your behavior," Bush said.

Changing hearts and changing behavior: This emphasis reveals a covenantal orientation, and lies at the heart of Bush's commitment to "compassionate conservatism," an agenda that is based on the belief that the greatest hope for the poor is found not in reform but in redemption. In every instance where Bush's administration sees a responsibility to help people, Bush has promised to look first to faith-based organizations, charities, and community groups that have shown their ability to save and change lives. Marvin Olasky, the Texas professor and Bush ally who coined the phrase "compassionate conservatism," believes that poverty is not caused by a lack of money, but by a lack of moral values on behalf of the poor.

"I understand the power of faith," said Bush to the volunteers in a Cleveland church in May 2001, "that faith can change lives." Along with Olasky, he believes that helping people with the greatest need is best done through some type of religious transformation — a conviction he first acted upon as Governor of Texas, when he allowed proselytizing Christian organizations to offer state-funded social programs, including a ministry-run prison program. George W. Bush is clearly an Abraham character who uses his position as president to remind people of the importance of religious obligation and moral clarity. Bush has "proven himself," said the Reverend Lou Sheldon of the "Traditional Values Coalition" to the September 4, 2004, *Washington Post*. "He supports a constitutional amendment [banning gay marriage]. He signed a law banning partial-birth abortion. He supports abstinence education." Bush won his second term in part because of "values voters" — religious conservatives who oppose gay marriage and abortion. Exit polling on Election Day 2004 revealed that 22 percent of voters identified "moral values" as the primary factor in their vote, and they favored Bush by a ratio of 4 to 1. Bush fits the "Hard America" definition provided by Michael Barone — an America marked by competition, accountability, and very little coddling.

Moses and Abraham. Clinton and Bush. Neither should be thought of as a superior religious leader — only different. In fact, the dual influences of Moses and Abraham are found throughout the Bible to have separate but equally valuable contributions to make, and the themes of exodus and covenant reveal themselves again and again over the course of the ministry of Jesus Christ. In a story found in the Gospel of Matthew, Jesus encounters a Canaanite women, a person who is clearly not a participant in God's covenant with the Israelites. At first, Jesus does not want to deal with her, since he feels that he was sent "only to the lost sheep of the house of Israel" (Matthew 15:24). But she persists in asking for his help, believing strongly that Jesus the Messiah could liberate her daughter from the grip of a demon. Finally Jesus, impressed by the woman's great faith, grants her wish and heals her daughter. This reveals the theme of exodus, with God acting to liberate all types of people from physical and spiritual bondage.

But covenant is also present in the ministry of Christ, most notably in the words of Jesus at the Last Supper, "This cup is the new covenant in my blood. Do this, as often as you drink it, in remembrance of me" (1 Corinthians 11:25). Then, in the anonymous Letter to the Hebrews, Jesus Christ is described as "the mediator of a better covenant" (Hebrews 8:6). Clearly, the early Christians saw themselves as people of covenant right along with the ancient Israelites. Both exodus and covenant, personified by the characters Moses and Abraham, have been carried by Christians and Jews into the present.

The challenge for American leaders and citizens is to strike a healthy balance between covenant and exodus, for both are integral parts of an authentic, deep, and lively religious faith. We run into trouble when we give priority to covenant, and in so doing downplay God's powerful work of liberation. At the same time, it is wrong to focus only on exodus, and in the process forget some of the obligations of covenant. A mature faith sees value in both obligation and liberation, and it embraces the importance of both

41

moral clarity and heartfelt charity. Both Moses and Abraham understood this, and displayed it in their own life stories. Moses was not only the liberator of his people, but also the law-giver (Exodus chs. 19-24). And, Abraham not only made a covenant with God, but walked in faith into an unknown future, which had the effect of elevating belief in the Lord above works of the law (Romans ch. 4).

Our political leaders have a sense of this as well, despite their tendency to lean toward one extreme or the other. "I don't think I could do my job as president," Bill Clinton said in a March 1994 ABC interview, sounding a lot like Abraham, "much less continue to try to grow as a person in the absence of my faith in God and my attempt to learn more about what it should be and grow." And George W. Bush expressed a Moses-like concern for helping the oppressed when he praised a group of Catholic volunteers in May 2001, saying, "God has a special concern for the poor. For some people, Jesus' admonition to care for the least of these is an admirable moral teaching. For the folks at this center, and centers like it all around America, it's a way of life."

Somewhere, between extreme devotion to either covenant or exodus, there is a healthy balance to be found. In fact, by holding the two in creative tension, leaders and citizens can benefit from the best of both concepts: The liberation, charity, and solidarity of the exodus ... plus the moral strength, clarity, and promise of the covenant. Belief in covenant and exodus is powerful when the two are held together, but problems can arise when one is given priority over the other. Witness the moral blindness of Bill Clinton in the Monica Lewinsky affair, and the lack of Christian charity shown by George W. Bush in his pattern of tax cuts that disproportionately favor the rich.

The challenge for church leaders is to focus on issues of obligation and liberation without being seen as pushing a partisan political agenda, or supporting a particular candidate. In July of 2004, the General Assembly of the Presbyterian Church (USA) did something I found troubling — it issued a resolution condemning the invasion of Iraq as "unwise, immoral, and illegal." In this case, it wasn't the assembly's weighing in on a public issue that bothered me, since it does so almost every year. Nor was it the church's stand against the war — I had questioned the invasion myself.

What took me aback was the stridency of the language. As soon as I heard it, I had the feeling it would cause problems in the pews. It didn't seem like the kind of statement that would inspire constructive conversation about a complex and controversial issue, or encourage dialogue about the competing claims of obligation and liberation, covenant and exodus.

While people certainly come to church to receive clear moral guidance, I am aware that they also come to engage in dialogue about difficult questions, and to find something that isn't readily available in the larger society — a place where disagreement is handled gracefully and respectfully by people of shared religious values. Because this resolution stressed one point of view, I feared it would have a polarizing effect. It was a divider, not a uniter.

Sure enough, within a day of the resolution, I began to hear complaints from church members, especially active-duty or retired members of the armed forces. To them, the assembly's action had drawn a line in the sand. Some supporters of the war even began to talk about leaving the church. "If the line is drawn as a result of the convictions of the majority, then okay," observed my parishioner, Mike Nelson, a career Air Force officer, fighter pilot, and Vietnam combat veteran. But Mike said he doubted that the assembly was speaking for the majority of Presbyterians.

Although I had been encouraging people to ask questions about the wisdom of the invasion since before American forces entered Iraq, I objected to this resolution because it did nothing to help my church members figure out what it means to be a follower of Christ in a time of war. It gave them no opening to discuss their concerns and wrestle with the conflicting feelings that arise at such a time. I knew that some members supported the war because they believed that the invasion was an effort to liberate the oppressed Iraqi people. Others opposed the military campaign because they could not reconcile it with their Christian obligation to practice nonviolence. But the Presbyterian pronouncement that the war was "unwise, immoral, and illegal" did nothing to encourage conversation about these issues or invite church members to perform a balancing act between various points of view. Parishioners are never helped by resolutions that force people to be either insiders or outsiders, driven even further apart in a society that's already politically polarized.

Lately, I see this happening again and again, whether the issue is war in Iraq, homosexuality, abortion, stem-cell research, or the Israeli-Palestinian conflict. Although Presbyterians enjoy freedom of conscience and aren't bound by these resolutions, many people object to having their donations used by a national body to send messages that don't represent their individual or congregational views. At the same time, people are struggling with these difficult issues, and they are looking for the church to teach, inform, and inspire them — to lead them with its pronouncements, instead of driving them away. So there's a tension between the perspective of the individual and the view of the church. This can be healthy and creative, but only when church pronouncements are firmly grounded in the Bible and theology, and are seen as being fair and nonpartisan.

This is, of course, easier said than done. Part of the problem with church pronouncements is that they are often too hastily made. My colleague, Susan Andrews, pastor of Bradley Hills Presbyterian Church in Bethesda, Maryland, and a former leader of the General Assembly, believes that pronouncements have to be carefully written and carefully studied. When this effort is made, she says, the resolutions "can help put theological and biblical foundations to what would otherwise be just political statements."

The Presbyterian Church, along with many other Christian bodies, has long believed it's important to take stands on public issues of moral concern. In 1958, the General Assembly declared that it had a responsibility "to speak on social and moral issues for the encouragement and instruction of the Church and its members." Past Presbyterian pronouncements have supported public school desegregation (1954), equal rights for women (1983), divestment in South Africa to help end apartheid (1985), a ban on land mines (1995), and reduction of greenhouse gases (1998) — positions that were once controversial, but are now accepted by many if not most Americans.

The question, then, is not *whether* to speak, but *how*. In this regard I've learned a great deal from Gerry Creedon, pastor of St. Charles Borromeo Catholic Church in Arlington, Virginia, and chairman of the Diocesan Peace and Justice Commission. Before the outbreak of the Iraq war, he developed a one-day program for his parishioners to talk and reflect on the church's analysis of war, which he conducted on three separate occasions to groups numbering between thirty and sixty participants. He also distributed the program to seventy parishes in the diocese.

The way it worked was this: After prayer, Gerry asked the participants to offer their reasons for either supporting or opposing military action in Iraq. He then gave a presentation on Catholic teaching on war and peace, including both just-war tradition and the older tradition of nonviolence. The program ended with a clear biblical challenge to work for peace, but it took no political stand — instead, it provided parishioners with an opportunity to engage in dialogue and listen to the voice of the Catholic tradition.

Such an approach can have great practical benefit in the life of a church, because its focus is on parishioners listening to one another instead of reacting to one another. In this case, a full analysis of the Iraq issue came out of the contributions of the participants themselves, and arguments were made for liberation and obligation in a clear and non-polarizing way.

I am convinced that dialogue is an essential part of the educational process, because it draws people into an issue in a way that the simple proclamation of traditional truths never can. It also reduces the resistance and defensiveness most people feel when presented with one side of an issue without an opportunity to reply, which often happens when a sermon is preached. "There is no easy way to respond to the remarks in a Sunday homily," says my friend Dan Napolitano, a Roman Catholic layman. "The priest has a 'bully pulpit' in every sense of the expression."

Dan has no problem with priests and ministers having political positions of their own, but he feels it's important for them to create a climate for multiple opinions and to avoid the mistake of assuming that their congregations are monolithic audiences. "Priests and ministers must preach to and lead a wildly diverse group," he says, "parishioners who are either with the NRA or ACLU, those who want the 'old days' and those who can't stand them, those who love the services and those who are ambivalent."

Diversity is a characteristic of every congregation, with fans of Bill Clinton sitting side by side with supporters of George Bush, and if we pastors don't acknowledge this and foster dialogue, we'll simply drive our parishioners further apart. In my own preaching, I try to lift up ideas and questions that will stimulate conversation, instead of shutting it down. I attempt to invite members from across the political spectrum to look at important matters along with me, and continue the conversation after the service is over. For some people, church may be the only place where this kind of discussion is possible — and even encouraged.

Adam Hamilton, the pastor of a large Methodist congregation in Leawood, Kansas, takes the use of dialogue in preaching even further. He recommends that preachers begin their sermons on tough issues by presenting an opposing position — and present it so powerfully that the congregation would believe that it is the preacher's own position if the sermon abruptly ended. Then, and only then, should preachers present their own positions, and they should take care to keep their arguments grounded in the Bible. As difficult as this approach may be, it creates an atmosphere of dialogue, and stands a better chance of actually changing minds than a more confrontational approach.

Of course, for every minister and every church, there will be times when they must articulate a position with absolute clarity. During the Civil Rights Era, the pastor of Fairfax Presbyterian delivered such a call for racial equality, but in most of the complex controversies we face today, there is no real benefit in rushing quickly to decide a matter with a church vote. Linda Olson Peebles, a minister at the Unitarian Universalist Church of Arlington, Virginia, believes that forcing a vote on contentious issues can make the minority feel marginalized. And when debates fixate on questions of wording and minor details, then people are pulled away, she says, from "the core faith stances that do in fact guide us."

It is a focus on these "core faith stances" that will enable churches to make their greatest contributions, and pastors can help their people to move toward Christian clarity by inviting them to engage in dialogue about the examples of Abraham and Moses in the face of a variety of contemporary issues. I am afraid that the church will continue to polarize its members if it forces them to take particular political stands, but it will draw people together if it begins to lift up current controversies — war, abortion, homosexuality — and discuss them in light of obligation and liberation, moral clarity and Christian charity, covenant and exodus.

These categories are helpful because they are not designed to win political arguments. Instead, they put us in touch with our core faith stances, and provide us with a clearer understanding of ourselves, the community of faith, and the larger culture. It is the interplay of obligation and liberation that helps us figure out what it means to be followers of Christ in America today, and this interplay is best experienced through dialogue with people who take their stands — with passion, commitment, and good faith — at various points along the spectrum that runs from Abraham to Moses.

Chapter Four

Separation Is For The Church,
Not The State

The Senate chaplain opens every workday of the U.S. Senate with a prayer. He provides pastoral care to senators and staff members, and is available to all workers — from cooks to committee chairpersons — some 6,000 people in and around the Senate. In addition to performing marriages and funerals, he is known for leading Bible studies, counseling people on ethical issues, and being supportive and helpful to all. When the current chaplain retires, I believe that his position should be abolished.

Yes, that's right: Abolished. Having a federally-funded chaplain is good for neither the church nor the state.

From a theological standpoint, it is hard to defend the existence of the Senate chaplain. Jesus never showed much interest in the kingdoms of this world, and the separation of church and state has always been better for the church than for the state. "Senators need prayer," says Stanley Hauerwas, a professor of theological ethics at Duke Divinity School, "but government ought not pay for it. Where the queen's coin comes, the queen is not far behind. The Senate chaplain gives legitimacy to a set of practices that has nothing to do with the worship of the Christian God."

The chaplain is an Abrahamic figure, speaking with clarity about the obligations and responsibilities of faithful people in government service. Unfortunately, his prayers in the Senate can give the impression that God's will is being done by the legislative process, a dubious proposition no matter what one's political views. His words also imply a close fit between being an American and being Christian, which is not necessarily true, especially in times of war. Hauerwas argues that prayer and scripture reading can be done correctly only in a community of faith — something the

49

Senate is not. The primary deity worshiped on the Senate floor, says Hauerwas, is Mars, the god of war. He adds, "Mars is a god I detest as a Christian."

Of course, some might argue that the federal government needs to hear a clear word from the Lord. If only this were allowed! In 1994, a Southern Baptist chaplain with the U.S. Air Force was forced to retire from the armed services because he had publicly criticized the morality of the 1991 war in the Persian Gulf. This chaplain, a former Vietnam War combat pilot named Garland Robertson, had written a letter to the editor of the *Abilene Reporter-News* in which he questioned the necessity of using force against the Iraqis. His public dissent from official war policy prompted numerous clashes with his superiors, resulting in an honorable discharge from the service. "I thought we [chaplains] were here to represent the faith traditions," Robertson told Ecumenical News International, "and I thought we were contributing to that goal. But the real issue that's brought out is that the chaplain is here to serve the [military] institution, and that's sad."

The very same is true for the Senate chaplain. Although he is hired to represent God, he would be quickly fired if he behaved like Moses, confronted Pharaoh, and publicly dissented from the positions of the government. The first amendment to the Constitution guarantees that "Congress shall make no law respecting an establishment of religion, or prohibiting the free exercise thereof," but it is impossible for that exercise of religion to be completely free when it is being funded by taxpayer dollars. Stanley Hauerwas'"Where the queen's coin comes, the queen is not far behind," is a lesson learned all-too-well by Air Force chaplain Garland Robertson. The separation of church and state is valuable not because it protects the state from the church, but because it keeps the church free of governmental interference.

Other constitutional problems arise around the funding of the Senate chaplaincy, specifically whether or not this is "an establishment of religion" prohibited by the Constitution. "Public money is used to set up the office," noted Robert Boston of Americans United for Separation of Church and State, when I spoke with him in 1994.

"No one should be taxed to support religion. I thought we got rid of state-supported religion with the Bill of Rights."

Then there is the practical question of how any one person — religious chaplain or secular counselor — can meet the needs of an increasingly diverse group of senators, staff members, and workers. It is true that the current chaplain, Barry C. Black, is an African-American Seventh Day Adventist, but his selection in the year 2003 broke new ground in the area of diversity. All of the chaplains since the creation of the position in 1789 had been white males, and most had been from mainline Protestant denominations such as the Episcopal, Methodist, and Presbyterian churches. Black's predecessors, Richard Halverson and Lloyd John Ogilvie, were Presbyterians, and as such they represented only about four percent of the United States population.

"My concern is that we live in a religiously diverse and pluralistic culture," says Mary Hunt, theologian and co-director of the Women's Alliance for Theology, Ethics, and Ritual in Silver Spring, Maryland. "To have a chaplain representing the dominant religious culture is no longer adequate." She suggests that if the Senate is going to have a chaplain at all, diversity should be a hallmark, and a variety of religious leaders should serve in this capacity, freeing the chaplaincy from bondage to one particular understanding of religious covenant. There is no reason that senators and staffers cannot be served by their own pastors, like everyone else.

If the position of Senate chaplain is abolished, the chaplain's $133,800 salary could be liberated from this obligation and put to good use elsewhere. Local clergy might make themselves available to meet pastoral needs in the Senate (much as they do in community hospitals), and if a daily prayer is truly desired by U.S. senators, they can invite their local ministers, priests, rabbis, and other religious leaders to offer invocations. Or, better yet, the senators can say prayers themselves, on a rotating basis, since so many claim to be people of faith. Their prayers would be idiosyncratic and sectarian, for sure, but such is the nature of religious devotion in a pluralistic society. With prayers being said voluntarily by local clergy and members of Senate, we could at least be confident that religion was being practiced freely, untouched by the long, strong arm of the federal government.

The fate of the Senate chaplain is an esoteric concern, but church-state issues are not — they are felt every day at the community level, far from the hallowed halls of the U.S. Capitol. Members of local congregations are bound to feel a temptation to break down the wall of separation between church and state, a desire that flares up most intensely when parish budgets are tight. Churches need lots of cash, you see — including funds to support tutoring programs, food banks, homeless shelters, and other social service projects in the larger community. But the fact is that voluntary contributions for such programs are largely discretionary, and when church budgets get lean, money for mission projects is likely to be quickly siphoned into fixed expenses such as staff salaries and utilities. In my work in four separate parishes since the mid-'80s, I've seen wild fluctuations in the amount of money available for social service efforts.

Given this instability, you might expect most heads of congregations to sing the praises of "charitable choice" — the section of the 1996 federal welfare reform law that provides for partnerships between government and religious institutions. Under this provision, churches can apply for welfare money for their social service programs and inject a spiritual dimension into tax-supported public assistance. For instance, government-funded computer training classes taught by church volunteers may begin with prayer, and church mentors may speak of their faith in God as they lead formal job training programs. It's a program that a covenant-keeper would certainly love, since it makes clear that religious obligation is an integral element of personal transformation.

Many people are indeed enthusiastic about the possibilities charitable choice offers, not least among them Al Gore and George W. Bush, candidates in the 2000 presidential campaign who both spoke in favor of government and religious organizations working together to solve social problems. At Calvary Presbyterian in Alexandria, volunteer tutor, Bill Wilson, leapt at the idea that congregations should use government funding to enhance their Christian mission. "If there is a need, then why not have churches and other social institutions take advantage of it?" he asked me, adding emphatically, "And there is a need!"

Charitable choice may seem like a godsend, but I have my concerns. As in the case of the Senate chaplain, I worry about the damage that government can do to religion when the wall between church and state is breached. And I wonder whether communities of faith can remain vibrant volunteer organizations, with strong patterns of private giving, once they have grown accustomed to federal funding. I'm enough of a fan of the exodus to believe that churches are healthiest when they have been liberated from all forms of government interference.

I believe that the church-state divide is a benefit because it protects the sacred from the secular — not the other way around. Federal funding invariably comes with federal direction on how money can be used, and these requirements can come into conflict with the convictions of a congregation. Rabbi Jack Moline of Agudas Achim Congregation in Alexandria, for instance, foresees "all sorts of problems" were he to accept government money, given some of the unique circumstances under which his congregation operates. As he points out, the Jewish calendar, which requires that certain activities be suspended on the sabbath and holidays, does not mesh with the secular calendar. And Jewish dietary requirements are not negotiable in his building or at any synagogue-sponsored activity. He prefers to "just say no" to government largess rather than compromise such religious beliefs.

Federal requirements also often seem capricious and confusing. I applaud religious volunteers who act as mentors to welfare families, but I don't want to get involved in instructing them in the nuances of distinguishing between speaking about their own faith (allowed) and engaging in "proselytization" (forbidden). While I would be pleased if my own church members at Fairfax Presbyterian took a computer class at a neighboring house of worship, I don't know how I could tell if the prayers of instructors crossed the line into prohibited "sectarian worship" — a term highly subject to interpretation. And I certainly wouldn't want my parishioners to feel that participation in the prayers of an unfamiliar faith or religious tradition is an expected — although technically optional —

part of the price they have to pay for free instruction in word processing or computer software.

There are certainly many congregations that are working hard to make these new church-state partnerships function well. Charlottesville Abundant Life Ministries in Charlottesville, Virginia, is a church-based urban outreach program offering after-school tutoring, teen mentoring, adult job training, and Bible studies in a low-income neighborhood. It accepts some government funding for the secular dimension of its ministry; for example, $20,000 in federal grants for teen programs. "When we can accept government funds without compromising our mission or religious identity, then we do so and count them a blessing, as they free up our private resources to further enhance our ministries," explains Amy Sherman, founder and former director of the project. Abundant Life Ministries uses government funds to liberate the oppressed, while maintaining its religious obligations — a graceful combination of exodus and covenant.

Sherman is grateful for the "faith-friendly climate" that has been created by charitable choice. But she, too, says that the group would rather lose funding and cut back programs "than to be found untrue to our Lord," and she thinks that not all religious organizations should take government funds, especially groups for whom conversion is absolutely central to their ministry approach. She gives the example of Teen Challenge, a nationwide youth drug abuse program that stresses relying on Christ's power in the effort to overcome addiction. While charitable choice might be attractive to followers of Abraham, such people are wise to draw the line when federal funding threatens to violate their covenant with God.

As church-based social-service ministries grow in budget and staff, I also fear they run the risk of becoming just another bureaucracy. Kevin Armstrong, acting director of a religion and urban culture project at the Polis Center, an academic research center in Indianapolis, has studied charitable choice and found that when congregations compete with secular social service agencies for funds, they begin to look more like social service agencies and less like congregations. He recalls one pastor's words after his congregation received its first grant check: "I wonder if my people still remember it's the Lord who provides." Armstrong challenges congregations to give back the money if the church's identity ever becomes compromised — if its covenant ever becomes corrupted.

Government funding can have a corrosive effect on an organization's budget. Give an organization a stream of extra money, and it soon comes to depend on it — a phenomenon not limited to congregations. A couple of former parishioners reminded me recently that when state lotteries were introduced, the income they produced was supposed to provide "the extras" not afforded by the regular budget. But today, in many cases, this money is desperately needed just to meet basic state functions and responsibilities.

For those organizations that can compartmentalize their programs — using government funds to underwrite computer classes and private money to fund biblically based life-skills classes — charitable choice can provide critical support for social-service ministries. In a sense, this kind of segregation of funds is really nothing new. "Government money is already deeply intertwined in many religious ministries in health care and a variety of social services," noted Father Bill Parent in 2000, when he served as coordinator of health care concerns for the Archdiocese of Washington. "Such funding has been justified by designating government money for non-religious purposes ... clinics for the poor in religious hospitals, church-run homeless shelters, or math textbooks for parochial schools." If groups can develop procedures to segregate their funds, federal dollars can be used to liberate the oppressed from illness and homelessness and ignorance, pleasing fans of the exodus without offending covenant-keepers.

But for local congregations that aren't large enough to compartmentalize their programs and deal with government reports and red tape, I say better to keep their hands off the federal funds. The vitality of our churches depends on the community's spirit of giving and participating, and it has long been my belief that people are most committed to activities that they choose to support with their disposable income — including church.

I have a hunch that there is at least some connection between active voluntary giving and high weekly church attendance (44 percent of the population) in America, compared with the low attendance in countries where church taxes have been assessed by the government, such as western Germany, where weekly attendance ranges from five percent to fourteen percent, according to a University of Michigan study. The healthiest churches are found in countries where congregations are liberated from governmental funding and control. When Moses delivered God's pronouncement to Pharaoh, saying, "Let my people go, so that they may celebrate a festival to me" (Exodus 5:1), he was speaking words that ring true even today.

Not that big federal bucks aren't attractive. Like most pastors, I would certainly welcome more financial support for my church programs, but I continue to believe that the "wall of separation" has served my congregations well. At Calvary Presbyterian, which I served for eleven years, we offered the "Eagle's Wings Tutoring Program," which matched at-risk students with volunteers for weekly one-on-one tutoring — and we did it without any government funding. I believe this enriched the program, because it challenged church members throughout the community to give of their own time, energy, and money. If Eagle's Wings had received a federal grant, I fear there would have been far less motivation for individuals to make a personal investment in it.

Kimberly Van Wagner, one of the tutoring coordinators for Eagle's Wings, agreed that without awareness of how government funding affects the community, critical volunteerism could be lost. "My observation is that once government money is introduced, the spirit of volunteerism can be hurt," she told me in 2000. "It is the spirit of reaching out and being part of the community that motivates many people to volunteer."

Some churches are skirting the minefields of charitable choice by forming partnerships with public institutions in ways that avoid church-state issues entirely. Since 1997, the Alexandria Tutoring Consortium has drawn volunteers from seventeen Protestant, Catholic, and Jewish congregations and sent them into public schools to help children with their reading. "There's too much red tape to cut through to have kids come into the churches," observes participant Fred Lyon, the co-pastor of Fairlington Presbyterian Church, "but there is hardly any the other way around." In this program, people make a faith-based decision to volunteer, but they don't include religious instruction in their efforts — their religious commitment is seen only in their concern for children in need. The Alexandria Tutoring Consortium has stepped over the church-state wall and been welcomed on the other side, because its volunteers are willing to work to help children in a completely secular setting. They are doing the work of Moses, without invoking Abraham at all.

In every program, however, it is imperative that roles and responsibilities be clearly defined, from the sacred side as well as the secular. Churches that choose to receive federal funding will have to find practical ways to compartmentalize their programs, so that government funds will be restricted to social service programs and private funds will be used for religious ministries. The great danger of charitable choice, it seems to me, is that it blurs the boundaries, creating the possibility that federal funds will be used for religious purposes and spiritual ministries will be corrupted into secular bureaucracies.

Even as more and more elected officials encourage sacred-secular partnerships, I remain convinced that there are good reasons to keep church and state separate — especially for congregations that want to pursue their ministries freely and remain vital and voluntary communities of faith. My warning to any church leader considering such a partnership would be: Never let yourself become so dependent on federal funds that you lose the spirit of generous voluntary giving. For the health of your congregation, do your best to resist the temptation of charitable choice. Now more than ever, communities of faith need freedom from the long, strong arm of the government, especially if they are going to remain true to their religious obligations as they do the important work of liberation. Separation of church and state can help the followers of Abraham to retain their sharp moral clarity, while also allowing the followers of Moses to maintain their passionate sense of charity.

This is not to say, however, that it is always easy to draw a bright line between where charitable action ends and political activity begins. Over the winter of 2005, Fairfax County, Virginia, faced an urgent need to house the homeless on freezing nights, including families with children who had been sleeping in wooded areas around Fairfax City. Area churches banded together to offer housing in church buildings, and a number of members of my church, Fairfax Presbyterian, joined this effort.

As a pastor, I always love to see my church members united by such a mission, but I wonder if opening the church as a shelter is really enough. Part of me wants to go further, to put effort into pressuring the local governments to build more shelters and affordable housing. Problem is, I've seen the difficulties that arise in my congregation when I ask whether Fairfax City, where my church is located, is doing enough for the homeless. Church members sense that I am wading into political waters, and their own political biases immediately surface. Liberals are anxious to go beyond charitable responses and work to change the system, but conservatives are suspicious of efforts that expand the role of government. While my congregation is united in its charitable desire to help the homeless, there is no consensus about what the church should do beyond providing a place of shelter.

Most church members simply don't like to see their pastor involved in politics. In 2004, a *Washington Post-ABC News* poll revealed that nearly two-thirds of Americans believe that religious leaders should not try to influence politicians' positions on issues. But Jesus himself had an impact on his society from the start of his ministry to its end, so any attempt to behave like him today is going to shake up the status quo, even if partisan politics are carefully avoided.

Fortunately, I do think politics can take a backseat to other concerns when churches make an effort to concentrate on promoting core Christian values, such as hospitality. Diana Butler Bass, author of *Broken We Kneel: Reflections on Faith and Citizenship*, has seen this at the Church of the Epiphany in downtown Washington, where she worships. Not long ago, her church started an effort to help the homeless by offering a simple Sunday breakfast, but then it expanded the activity into a full morning of worship, prayer, fellowship, and food that includes the whole congregation.

What originated as a feeding program has become an opportunity for homeless guests and church members to sit together, eat together, and share stories of their lives and their faith. This develops new awareness, and political positions can change. Bass, a Democrat, says that the experience at Epiphany has given her "both a greater appreciation for the traditions of Democratic social concern and sharpened their shortcomings — leading me to understand that a more creative, and more potentially challenging, set of political solutions is necessary to care for the least among us." She now recognizes that "no political party has the corner on addressing homelessness and urban poverty."

Experienced community organizers tell me that effective social action — the work of biblical liberation — has to begin with strong relationships across congregational and denominational lines. John Lentz, a pastor in Cleveland Heights, Ohio, reports that his suburban Presbyterian Church is beginning a relationship with an urban Baptist Church so that parishioners can share their experiences of pain and hopefully discover mutual self-interest in a variety of difficult social issues. "We know in Cleveland Heights that unless we engage ourselves in justice for East Cleveland, the drugs and the poverty are just down the hill and creeping up," he tells me. "It's in our long-term self-interest to do this."

In recent years, I have been working with an interfaith group to organize a religious network in Northern Virginia. This multi-faith, multiracial group — made up of blacks, whites, Christians and Jews, and probably Republicans as well as Democrats, conservatives and moderates as well as liberals — is determined to be a civic voice that can balance the political and business voices in the region. But the organizers have stressed the importance of developing personal relationships across racial and denominational barriers, and to build a foundation of understanding and trust before we begin to identify the issues we need to address. We know that there may not be much in common, politically, between black urban pastors and white suburban pastors, a disconnect that could pose problems when particular issues arise in one region or another. But if we form deeply personal relationships, then we pastors will trust and support one another and we'll be able to avoid political divisions.

Gerry Creedon, the pastor of St. Charles Borromeo Catholic Church in Arlington, Virginia, believes that this approach is essential, that we need to find a way through conservative and liberal ideological frameworks "to an underlying experience of faith." Then later, when our network begins to work on particular issues — affordable housing, perhaps, or immigration — I hope it will be able to avoid political tensions because we'll all be looking at these concerns through a broader lens as questions of human dignity and social justice, rather than worrying about how we label our approach to solving them.

Unless they identify and embrace shared principles, faith communities will shatter along political lines. These unifying principles can be as simple as seeking justice and ending hunger — core stances that have shaped the work of Bread for the World (BFW), a nationwide Christian citizens' movement, for the past thirty years. I've been involved with BFW since I was in college and seminary, and I have always found it to be a faithful, nonpartisan voice on legislation that deals with hunger issues both here and abroad. My colleague Roy Howard, pastor of St. Mark Presbyterian Church in Rockville, Maryland, points out that BFW has both Republicans and Democrats — from former GOP presidential candidate Bob Dole to former Clinton administration budget director Leon Panetta — on its board of directors, and its leaders "are very careful to stay focused on their mission to make social policy that helps the hungry" and to speak with a unified Christian voice.

Of course, strong relationships and shared principles are no guarantee of perfect unity. At Calvary Presbyterian Church in Alexandria, where I served as pastor for eleven years, I worked hard to develop bonds between African immigrants and Americans, and attempted to create a climate of hospitality within the congregation, but the church still experienced divisions. I don't doubt that as I move ahead with the homeless coalition and the interfaith network, I'll face some criticism at Fairfax Presbyterian — there will always be proponents of religious obligation who see Christian social action as being partisan, or political, or outside the core mission of the church, which they define as concentrating on nourishing the soul and enforcing moral clarity. But, I can live with this kind of resistance. As one of my mentors, Ed White, a consultant at the Alban Institute, says, "If we cannot do anything unless we all agree, the church is immobilized."

60

David Ensign, the pastor of Clarendon Presbyterian Church in Arlington, Virginia, finds it helpful to remind his church members that much of scripture is inherently political. For example, he says, the Moses story is not only about God, but also about the politics of liberation, "about speaking truth to power." He knows that there will always be people who disagree on policy and on partisan politics, but such disagreement should never be an excuse for inaction, because inaction amounts to a blessing of the status quo — and that, of course, is a political act in itself.

To me, it's important to avoid being part of a paralyzed church, because I know that so much bad can happen when good people choose to do nothing. And so I'll push ahead with the work of liberation, remembering that the key to avoiding political conflict is to develop strong relationships across partisan lines, and to use clear biblical principles as the foundation for any form of Christian social action. The liberation of the exodus does not have to conflict with the obligations of the covenant, especially if time and effort is put into building a community that can speak with the voice of the church — as opposed to the state — on a range of pressing social issues.

Chapter Five

Finding Room In God's House

"My oldest daughter was married from that church; my husband was buried from that church." The voice on the radio was choking up with emotion. "I put a lot of money, a lot of hard work, a lot of time into that church, and I hate the idea of people of that ..." the speaker paused "... moving in like that. And I don't feel like it's my home church anymore."

In my living room, I listened with a mixture of fear and fascination to the words being broadcast by WAMU. "That church" was Calvary Presbyterian in Alexandria, the congregation I served as pastor from 1989 to 2000, and the speaker was a woman who has been a member of the congregation since 1955. I had spoken with her privately about her concerns, but it was startling to hear her anguish aired publicly, as part of a 1996 National Public Radio feature on Calvary's changing racial and cultural identity.

We were a formerly all-white church with 125 Ghanaian immigrants in a congregation of 350 adults, and our changing composition had altered the way we worshiped. One particular African-style service had deeply offended my parishioner's sense of dignity. Offerings were brought forward with song and swirling dance, accompanied by drums, synthesizer, and electric guitar. "If they want to worship that way," I heard her say, "fine with me. But don't bring it into my sanctuary. They were running up and down the aisle, hollering 'I'm happy, I'm happy,' waving a white flag. Well, as I say, if they want to do that, that's their business. But why do I have to sit and listen to it?"

Across America, immigrants are coming to church, just as they always have, and congregations such as Calvary are trying to find room for them in God's house. But where previous waves of immigrants were largely European, these new arrivals are coming from non-western countries with cultures and skin colors more discomforting to white Americans than that of Europeans. The missionaries our churches sent to Africa, Asia, and Latin America were successful beyond their wildest dreams: Those who heard their preaching are now coming to the United States and starting or joining churches here. These newcomers are often more openly passionate about the faith than are native-born Americans, and they shake up established churches by introducing new worship styles and beliefs.

It's been my experience that some American church members love these changes, and they celebrate the liberation of the church from racial segregation and traditional European worship styles. One of our elders said at the African-style service that he had "never felt the presence of the Spirit so strongly." But others feel a profound sense of loss, and are driven by an obligation to maintain the traditional terms of their relationship with God. My parishioner on the radio was clearly experiencing loss of comfort, tradition, and control in the church in which she had long worshiped, and she mourned the corruption of what must have been, for her, a pure form of traditional worship.

Diversity versus purity is yet another way to describe the liberation-obligation dichotomy, and it is one that creates a particularly tricky balancing act for leaders of the church. An enormous challenge for pastors today is to provide quality pastoral care to members who are threatened by change, even as we help our congregations incorporate the immigrants who increasingly will fill our pews.

Economic and political chaos in Africa has led to an increase in emigration, a trend that will surely continue. By the mid-90s in Alexandria, three Ghanaian groups were worshiping within a two-mile radius: one Pentecostal, one Seventh-day Adventist, one Presbyterian. These immigrants bring with them true evangelistic zeal, sparked by the phenomenal growth of the church in Africa. That continent's Christian population rose from 8.5 million in 1900 to 285.7 million in 1993, according to David Barrett, a statistician specializing in churches. He estimates that the number of African Christians will reach 760.1 million by 2025.

In the next generation, we may see a flow of missionaries not to Africa, but out of Africa. Stephen Nkansah, an evangelist trained in Ghana who joined Calvary in 1993, started the Ghanaian Presbyterian Fellowship, which was responsible for most of Calvary's African growth. In the American Catholic Church, fewer and fewer men are answering the call to the priesthood, but in Africa, the number of seminarians has almost quadrupled over the past 25 years.

Our country continues to hold a strong attraction for Latin Americans as well. There are now 26 million Hispanics in the United States, many of whom are Catholic. David Early, a spokesman for the United States Catholic Conference, predicts that "by 2010, the majority of Catholics in the United States will be of Hispanic descent." Many parishes now have Spanish-speaking priests to meet this demand, and Cardinal Roger Mahoney of Los Angeles requires all new priests in his archdiocese to be able to speak Spanish. The St. Anthony of Padua parish in Northern Virginia offers six masses: three in English, three in Spanish. Mariachi bands contribute to the liturgy in many congregations.

Christians are also pouring in from Asia. After Latinos, Filipinos are the largest immigrant group in the American Catholic Church. Korean churches are popping up all over, often sharing space with American congregations but maintaining a separate identity (witness the number of Korean signs in front of Protestant churches in urban areas). Christianity in Korea is a real Presbyterian success story: American missionaries took the gospel to the country in the 1800s, and by 1997 there were between six million and eight million Presbyterians in Korea — twice the number in America.

It's important to note that not all immigrants are diversity-hungry proponents of the exodus; many are as concerned with purity of worship and community as the most passionate American covenant-keepers at Calvary Presbyterian Church. When immigrant Christians reach the United States, they either form a new congregation or join an established church; the former is the Protestant norm, the latter more common among Catholics. There are an estimated 7,000 Latino congregations in the United States, and as many as 3,000 Korean immigrant churches. This number could easily soar into the tens of thousands, however, since these churches are often informally organized and hard to count. Calvary has a small, Spanish-speaking Pentecostal church meeting in its basement, and I doubt it appears on any "official" list of churches.

The desire to worship in their own language is what first motivates purity-conscious newcomers to form separate congregations. A second motivation is cultural transmission: Making a church is a way of creating a community within which children can be brought up in the traditions their parents want to pass on. Of course, when these traditions run counter to American sensibilities, conflict can arise. In the early 1990s, Calvary rejected a request to share its space with a Korean Presbyterian congregation, in large part because the Koreans refused to ordain women as elders.

Concerns arise on the immigrant side as well. For example, the theologies of American Protestant Christianity often seem excessively modernized to these foreigners. African Christians are puzzled by discussions of issues such as the ordination of gays and lesbians. They were raised to think of homosexuality as an abomination, and they wonder why the American Church would even consider being open to such a sexual orientation. At Silver Spring Presbyterian Church in Silver Spring, Maryland, the church's desire to be inclusive of gays and lesbians has created tension between African immigrants (who now make up more than eighty percent of the congregation) and progressive white members, who include gays and parents of gay children. The African concern for purity is not easily reconciled with ever-increasing American tolerance of sexual diversity.

There are other differences as well. As immigrants arrive in large numbers, they are "creating a younger, more colored, and more conservative Protestant Christianity," according to Stephen Warner, a professor of sociology at the University of Illinois at Chicago who has studied immigrant churches. Their conservatism is theological, not political; they do not necessarily agree with American conservatives on social policy. Warner observes that Catholic parishes are "becoming more Hispanicized — more devotional. The statues that were removed from churches after Vatican II are returning."

Sadly, immigrants sometimes form separate churches because many established churches will not accept them. They go looking for a congregation that is charitable and comfortable with cultural diversity, but then they run into barriers set up by clarity-obsessed cultural purists. Nkansah tells the story of a cab driver friend who took a fare to Potomac, in Montgomery County, Maryland, and then decided to attend a service at a Baptist Church in that area. He walked in — and the congregation phoned the police, describing him as a trespasser. He said, "No, I am a Baptist, from Ghana." They insisted he was trespassing. Cameroonian Sam Takunchung recalls that the First Christian Church of Lubbock, Texas, refused to serve him communion, even though the pastor had just intoned the words, "This is Jesus Christ's table, people shall come from everywhere to it."

More subtle forms of rejection occur when an American Church misunderstands — with all good intentions — what immigrants want. "I know and love Africans," says the Reverend Thomas Rook, former missionary in Cameroon and associate pastor of Fourth Presbyterian Church in Chicago, but "to know Africans is to know people with problems — money problems, family issues, passport and visa concerns." In his eyes, Africans are defined by what they need. Yet some Africans leave churches like Fourth Presbyterian because they are not given sufficient opportunity to serve — they want to give as well as receive. James Acquaah left Fourth Presbyterian to become part of Ebenezer, a church formed in the mid-90s for Africans, because he thought he could better help an immigrant church. "If you are in a church, and you don't have much to do," he reflects, "eventually you get bored. But here I am very much involved."

So, what hope is there for the successful incorporation of immigrants into American Churches? Can exodus-inspired diversity ever overcome covenant-keeping purity? At Calvary, our Ghanaian Presbyterian Fellowship brought newcomers into full active membership in the church, but we continued to meet resistance whenever an African-style offering was proposed. We had better results inviting Ghanaian pastors to assist me with communion, recruiting Africans to teach church school and serve as elders, and occasionally using conga drums to call the congregation to worship. On Easter 1997, our sanctuary choir was joined by the Ghanaian singing band, Nkansah helped me to lead worship, and the service was followed by an international potluck dinner. Perhaps one way to racial and cultural harmony is through the stomach.

The challenge for integrated churches is to create rituals and symbols that incorporate both the native and the immigrant experience, notes sociologist Nancy Ammerman of Hartford Seminary, and to help immigrants move into positions where they have the power to make decisions. The Catholic Church has been a leader in doing this. Years ago, parishes were established along ethnic lines, and worshipers would attend either a German Church, an Italian Church, or an Irish Church. Purity was seen as being more important than diversity, and it was certainly more satisfying to members of the immigrant groups themselves. Today, however, bishops are working to bring newcomers into established parishes, and pastors are putting immigrants on parish councils so that their churches will be forced to deal with ethnic differences and, with any luck, be enriched by them.

"We of European descent can learn from immigrants' beliefs and practices," says Early, of the U.S. Catholic Conference, "and how they see faith and life as a whole. Their faith colors their entire existence." The newcomers deliver a challenge to Americans who see religious devotion as a Sunday-morning-only phenomenon, or as a limited commitment. Certainly the Hispanics who meet in Calvary's basement would worship seven nights a week if they were allowed to do so.

As difficult as it is to incorporate immigrants gracefully into established churches, doing so holds great promise for vital Christianity in the twenty-first century. Predominantly white mainline churches are declining in membership, but growth can come if they open their doors to the Africans, Latinos, and Asians moving into their neighborhoods. Of course, churches must set aside their attachment to cultural purity and be open to change — and to a more spirited style of worship — if they want to keep these newcomers. I'm convinced that the united congregations of every denomination will stand the best chance of holding onto the second generation of immigrants, a group that sees itself not as Ghanaian or Salvadoran or Korean, but as American.

Unfortunately, Calvary Presbyterian did not remain united long enough to provide ministry to this Americanized second generation. Concerns about purity, from both the African and the American perspectives, ended up trumping the desire for diversity. By 1999, Calvary's average attendance was close to 200 at the English-language morning service (up from 120 in 1989), and at least that number at the afternoon Ghanaian gathering, which was conducted in the Twi language and led by seminarian Nkansah, and the congregation began to wrestle with the question of whether to remain one congregation or split into two. Calvary tried to maintain some unity, with its "education hours," for example, but this led to overcrowding in the building and parking problems caused by the tripling or quadrupling of attendees on Sundays.

It would be disingenuous to suggest, though, that the tensions we began to experience were caused only by traffic snarls and scheduling snafus. We were drifting into separate camps, not pushed apart by hostility, but instead pulled apart by a natural human hunger for community with people of similar interests and background — in other words, purity. These were tensions I didn't fully appreciate when I first became excited about the growing diversity of the church, and I have to admit that I was loath to see the congregation divide.

But it wasn't something I knew how to stop — or even whether I should stop. Those who wanted to worship in English attended only the upstairs morning service, while those who desired the Twi experience showed up exclusively for what some African worshipers began to call "the downstairs church" — a phrase that not only reflected the location of the gathering, but also, I suspect, a keen sense of being under the authority of the established church.

So what was wrong with this picture? Nothing, some would say. Plenty of big Protestant Churches have two different services — or more. With the resources to offer a wide range of distinctive programs, some large congregations are doing very well. In the year 2000, more than one-half of America's Protestant worshipers were meeting in fourteen percent of the churches in the land, and the number of congregations that average more than 1,000 in attendance had grown to more than 8,000 (from only 93 in 1965).

Still, these so-called megachurches make up a tiny percentage of the nation's churches. According to the Barna Research Group, which publishes poll-based studies on contemporary church life, the majority of Protestant congregations remain small neighborhood churches. Another 25 percent, including Calvary, have between 200 and 400 members.

What bothered me at Calvary was the sense that I had failed in the multicultural goals that I had shared with many members of the congregation. One threat to our unity had been, quite simply, the differences in schedules between recent immigrants and long-term church members. Many of the newcomers take service jobs with evening hours, often working unpredictable shifts, sometimes on weekends. That means there is less chance that significant relationships will develop between newcomers and old-timers. "I am not an expert in multiculturalism," says Ken Pilkenton, an airline pilot who was a very active member of Calvary, "but have always found better understanding of others comes primarily from one-on-one and small-group contact."

Another even more important challenge stemmed from differing styles. New arrivals from Ghana brought with them the spirited Pentecostal style of worship that is sweeping a broad range of African denominations, as well as an organizational system that didn't always match our American form of church leadership. This tension was heightened for us by the fact that a Ghanaian "steering committee" had become a kind of shadow governing body within the church — doing good work among Ghanaians, to be sure, but not always communicating effectively with Calvary's elders. Not that we American-born church members were always clear in our messages to them, either.

Halfway through 1999, our board of elders and I decided that Calvary was no longer functioning as one community, and made the decision to create a "daughter congregation" called the Ghanaian Presbyterian "Mission" — the technical term for the first stage in the creation of any Presbyterian Church. I had come to think that two pure, healthy Presbyterian Churches would be better for the cause of Christianity than one diverse, unhappy congregation, and the majority of elders — American and African — agreed. The Ghanaian group, which began to meet at a nearby elementary school and gained the status of "church" in June 2003, is still being led by Nkansah, who is now a seminary graduate and ordained Presbyterian pastor.

Still, it was a painful move, especially for those Ghanaians who had to decide whether to stay at Calvary or go to the new mission church. American members who had worked hard for diversity thought it was a retreat or even a defeat. I began to feel strained relationships with many of the members I admire the most — people I had worked with for years, side by side, to make Calvary a more welcoming and inclusive place. "In my life, it was the greatest missed opportunity I have ever seen," reflected Peggy Severson, who had been a member of the church for twenty years. "God led the Ghanaians here for a reason. God wanted us to figure it out."

The bottom line for me is that no church can make its worshipers want what they don't want. Ghanaians who desire a Ghanaian-Church experience will seek out such a congregation, no matter how hospitable and multicultural a liberation-oriented American Church tries to be. American Presbyterians who crave traditional American worship will look for an obligation-oriented congregation that offers such a service, regardless of how spirit-filled are the praises of a Ghanaian singing band. Purity is a powerful draw, especially in the midst of a larger culture that is becoming increasingly diverse, unpredictable, amoral, and chaotic.

Size also matters, and I'm beginning to believe that "thinking small" is the key to healthy church life in the future, regardless of whether a congregation is segregated or multicultural. There is evidence that megachurches are now experiencing slower growth rates, due in part to their lack of personal connection and intimacy. Some of them are responding by looking for ways to become more intimate internally — establishing sub-groups, redesigning worship spaces to facilitate conversation, and, like Calvary, setting up offshoot churches. "As the church grows larger, the church must grow smaller," reflects Pierce Klemmt, rector of Christ Church in

Alexandria, a 3,000-member Episcopal congregation that averages 1,200 worshipers each Sunday. "Whatever you do," he says, "meet in small groups" — groups that can act like small churches.

In retrospect, I feel a sense of peace with Calvary's solution. I'm aware of one Florida congregation, the Orlando Community Church, that now intentionally establishes a new church whenever its membership reaches 340. It's a "multichurch" instead of a megachurch, operating on the assumption that a number of intimate communities of faith can do as much good as one large, program-rich corporate congregation.

But does this mean that we have given in to the often-lamented tribalism that is sweeping our world today? I hope not. I can only say that these types of choices are going to continue to shape the church in the new century. Diversity of cultures and disparity in lifestyles and schedules are going to force people to make more and more decisions about the character, time, and language of their worship services, and along with these choices will come concern about purity — and divisions along cultural lines. Recently, a group of Korean Churches pulled out of our regional church body — National Capital Presbytery — to form their own Korean-language presbytery, and other immigrant churches are being planted in this country as mission churches of their home denominations — not as American congregations. Whether their tribe is American or Ashanti, most people are looking for familiarity and a certain amount of purity when they come to church.

The good news is that attendance at Calvary's English-language worship service did not drop when the Ghanaian congregation was created, which told me that we had already become two distinct groups. And despite the fact that Twi-language worship and education was being offered at a new location, a good number of Ghanaians stayed at Calvary, preserving its multicultural identity. A visitor had to be comfortable with diversity to feel at home there, and someone who desired a more homogeneous group would do better elsewhere. But with strong and committed members in both locations, the future was looking bright not only for Calvary, but for its daughter congregation as well.

72

Churches that want to work with immigrants have a choice to make: Follow Moses on the path of liberation, or Abraham on the road of obligation. Followers of Moses will have to embrace the fact that they are participating in a true exodus, and that they will be walking a rough and rocky road toward the promised land of racial and cultural diversity. Practical steps for these congregations include: Inviting immigrant pastors to participate in the leadership of worship; finding ways to eat together and share cultures at international potluck dinners; electing immigrants to positions of leadership; and building understanding through one-on-one and small group contact. This is an exciting ride through the wilderness, and it's one that can expand an American congregation's appreciation of the richness of the universal body of Christ. In addition, it can help them to understand, perhaps for the first time, that the American Church belongs not to Americans, but to God.

Moses is not the only leader to consider when looking for guidance in this area. Followers of Abraham can also work across racial and cultural boundaries, but their focus needs to be on covenant-keeping and true respect for the purity of each community's worship and theology. American Churches that take this path should consider hosting an immigrant congregation within their building, or giving financial support to a "daughter congregation" that offers worship in another language. According to the theory that the church can grow larger, externally, by growing smaller, internally, there is no reason to believe that a healthy Christian community cannot be made up of several cultural groups. As long as acceptance of another Christian group is genuine, and communication across racial and cultural boundaries is strong, it is entirely possible that several distinctive congregations will be able to serve God in a complementary fashion.

In fact, many Christians — whether they were born in Africa or Asia or America — are claiming that they must preserve their distinctive cultures if they are to worship God with integrity. The church in America is, for them, a salad bowl instead of a melting pot, meaning that individual ingredients will keep their flavor and remain separate and distinct, instead of losing their individual qualities and becoming blended and indistinguishable. Finding room in

God's house suddenly requires an expanded vision of what this house looks like, and it calls us to remember that Jesus said, "In my Father's house there are many dwelling places" (John 14:2).

Clearly, we want to share the same house. But that doesn't always mean that we have to occupy the same room.

Chapter Six

Lessons In Virtue
That Books Can't Teach

There's no question, virtue is a hot topic these days. Walk around a bookstore or sign onto one of the online book services, and you'll see that over the past decade or two virtue has been the inspiration for literally hundreds of books. The most familiar is William J. Bennett's *Book of Virtues*, of course, and the former secretary of education has had another fifteen titles on the market, including tapes and children's books based on his bestseller.

Virtue's thrall goes well beyond annual book lists. Character education has become a popular component of many school curriculums; at least twelve states have passed policy statements on character education; the actor, Tom Selleck, perhaps better known as Magnum, P.I., has hosted a video program on character education for elementary schools.

I suppose we should be thankful. After all we hear and read about violence and vice, it's refreshing to see virtue become an industry all of its own, but I can't help thinking that most of these endeavors, no matter how well-intentioned, are lacking an essential element. The books and classes miss what I believe to be a central truth about virtue: It is learned from life, not lessons. Although we may think of virtue as being an obligation — with its links to purity, moral clarity, and personal responsibility — virtue also requires a certain type of liberation.

This is not to say that covenant-keeping can't be helpful in crafting good character. When I think of my own work as a minister, I realize how much I rely on the Old and New Testaments — also called the Old Covenant and the New Covenant — as a guide to virtuous behavior. But one of the greatest strengths of the Bible is that it is so much more than "A Treasury of Great Moral Stories"

(Bennett's subtitle). It teaches by example, by involving us in tales of individual lives and of people's evolving relationship with God. In fact, it's more like a book of role models. Think of Moses or King David or the Apostle Peter, whose stories reveal both their strengths and their all-too-human failings. They cannot be reduced to simple morality tales. But they clearly challenge us to embrace virtue and avoid vice.

People often look to their ministers for guidance about questions of character, and I've often wished I had easy answers — but I don't. In recent years, though, I've begun to realize that the answers are all around us, if we allow ourselves to be liberated from the lessons of good-vs.-evil morality tales. As we remembered the deaths of some active members of Calvary Presbyterian Church, I became more and more convinced that good character comes from observing and copying virtuous people, that it is developed through relationships in communities.

Among the members we lost was John Middlecoff, an usher who used to be a fixture at the church entrance. I thought of John as the "Cal Ripken" of Calvary, not only because he was proud of his Baltimore birthplace, but because he played his position at the door, week in and week out, rarely missing a day. He welcomed all comers to services, a living example of dependability and diligence. I don't mean to suggest that John was a perfect man. He wasn't. Nor did he set out to teach anyone good character. But his ways rubbed off on many of us whom he greeted with a sly smile — and a characteristic snapping of his suspenders for small children. Nobody could replace John — or quite pull off his suspender trick — but I saw several people try to fill the gap he left at the door. We miss our teachers when they are gone.

I'm hardly the first to wrestle with what virtue is all about. Aristotle thought of virtue as a state of character gained by repeatedly performing good actions. Thomas Hibbs, a contemporary philosopher who has taught at Boston College, calls virtue "an acquired excellence of character that renders a person capable over the long haul of behaving in certain reliable ways."

I think both Aristotle and Hibbs are onto something. Hibbs likens the acquisition of virtue to athletic training; both require repetition and hard work; both are most easily learned by following examples. Books and programs and covenants can be helpful, of course, but in the end, virtue is best learned by practice, not through abstract thought. As Hibbs points out, if you want to learn to shoot hoops, playing basketball beats reading a book about basketball.

Virtuous living is a team sport, not an individual activity. By that I mean it requires a community of accountability and support. That's why I think the Eagle's Wings Tutoring Program at Calvary succeeded in making a small difference in some local children's lives. The program matched volunteer tutors with neighborhood schoolchildren, many of whom came from chaotic homes. Meeting for an hour each week in the church basement, the children absorbed virtues of kindness, perseverance, and diligence from their tutors. Character is not so much taught as it is "caught," in a setting like that.

The St. Peter's School in Waldorf has adopted a rather different approach, one that is growing in popularity in public and private schools. This Catholic elementary school's character-formation program features a particular virtue — such as "self-control" — as the focus for each month. The children engage in projects and activities that help them to understand and live by virtue, and every subject is oriented to touch on the featured trait. Is it working? I asked the Reverend Bill Parent, who was associate pastor at St. Peter's Church. "The initial effect is that it gives the children language to talk about issues," he told me. Perhaps the program's greatest strength is that it involves sessions for the parents, and makes character development a priority for the school, church, and community.

I once visited an elderly woman84 recovering from a stroke in the hospital. I asked about her husband, and she lamented that he was "no good," that he never wanted their children to learn more than how to write their names. But she had stressed education for them, and now all four have made a success in careers ranging from business to academics. They imitated their mother, a virtuous woman, not their father. William Willimon, dean of the Chapel at Duke University, puts it succinctly: "Virtue is not following rules, but rather virtue begins by being good. Luther said

77

you don't get apples from a thorn bush and I agree, so far as people are concerned."

At its heart, virtue is not following rules — it is not a legalistic obsession with obligation, purity, moral clarity, and personal responsibility. Instead, virtue begins by being good, by putting one foot in front of the other and following a role model like Moses. It may require some wandering in the wilderness, but the final destination is a new and better land.

At Calvary, we had a practice of marking fiftieth wedding anniversaries in our services, and I learned from many members of the congregation that younger married couples saw these services as more than celebrations of a long marriage. "I think it's incredible that people can stay together this long," one member of the congregation told me. Debbie Noel had been married for eight years at the time, and had two children. "It gives me strength," she said. "If others can do it, then I hope I can, too." Senior teachers who have made it far down the road of married life (a road that invariably has its share of potholes) inspire young learners who will later become teachers themselves. "We become virtuous over a lifelong period of trial and error, self-knowledge, self-criticism, observation, correction, example," Willimon has told me. "The young need more opportunity to be with and to observe the old."

That's why the process of teaching and learning virtue is done best in families, churches, and businesses. Any community — whether it be small as a family or large as a school — can contain both teachers and learners who help each other to strive for excellence. Contrast that with the sort of initiatives several states have adopted — such as the act passed in Alabama in 1995 that requires students to receive ten minutes of instruction per day in character traits ranging from citizenship to sportsmanship, as well as to recite the Pledge of Allegiance. "You can't simply have virtue with a smiley face," Hibbs has told his students in Boston.

But what if people are reluctant to exchange a book of virtues for a community of flesh-and-blood human beings? The clarity of a book can be very attractive, especially when compared to the chaos of a congregation. Certainly not everyone wants to follow fallible human beings — people as flawed as Moses, who had the murder of an Egyptian on his criminal record (Exodus 2:11-12) — on a journey to an uncertain future. Some people understandably prefer the clear obligations of Abraham over the vague liberation promised by Moses.

In my experience, the life of the church has brought into focus a conflict that has become familiar in our multicultural society — a conflict between the virtue of tolerance and accepting differences, on the one hand (liberation), and the need to be true to particular beliefs and customs on the other (obligation). The examples in our society are many, some more profound than others. Should police officers be allowed to wear dreadlocks? Should homosexuals be allowed to be Boy Scout leaders? Should school testing take place on the sabbath? In each case, individual differences clash with institutional expectations, and different types of character formation occur depending on the path that is chosen.

The prevailing ethos these days is to accept, accommodate, and adapt to differences. The virtue in that liberating approach is evident in the vibrancy of our culture, from the range of foods at the sidewalk cafes to the varied traditions our children learn to appreciate — and the languages they hear — in class. There's no doubt in my mind that we all profit from learning about and adapting to such cultural differences. But each time we adapt, we also give something up. And, in the church, which is founded on a set of obligations and beliefs, figuring out what we should give up and what we should stick to can be particularly perplexing.

I struggle with these issues every day, and there is no book that can give me clear guidance. A friend once asked me to help him plan a memorial service for an acquaintance, with the understanding that most of the people attending would not be religious. I hardly knew where to begin. The secular world doesn't accept the ideas of resurrection inherent in Christian theology. Without a common language grounded in the Bible or religious practice, which words should I choose? Even though I was not going to take part in the service, I was struck by the tension in myself between exodus-style inclusiveness and covenant-oriented exclusiveness — between wanting to help plan an event that would welcome nonreligious participants and allow them to feel comfortable with the service, while preserving the essence of the Christian faith.

On another occasion, when I was asked by a Jewish bride to take down all the crosses in my sanctuary for her marriage to a Christian, I refused. She wasn't pleased, but she was asking me to be more flexible — more inclusive — than my faith would allow.

I am hardly alone in these balancing acts. Most religious leaders claim they want to be hospitable to all people in their programs, but they balk if they are asked to abandon a distinctive tradition or modify a long-standing belief. They have good reason: If they dump their distinctiveness, they lose the identity that gives them meaning in the first place. So they live with the tension of guarding their valuables while they throw open their doors.

Signs of this strain pop up constantly. The 1964 Civil Rights Act recognized the peculiar role of religious organizations and gave them the right to discriminate in their hiring — to employ only people who share their beliefs. Abraham would be proud. But should those organizations be allowed to continue such practices if they receive federal funds to carry out public programs? That issue sparked debate in relation to President Bush's "faith-based" initiative. Should the Salvation Army, which holds the belief that homosexual activity is a sin, be allowed to discriminate against gays in its hiring? While I am certainly not in favor of discrimination, I have to admit that a question is nagging me: If the effectiveness of the Salvation Army comes from uniformity of belief, isn't it logical that Salvation Army staff members be required to share the same convictions?

In this case, the argument should be for the virtue of inclusiveness, since the Salvation Army receives federal dollars and performs ministry for a broad cross section of the population. But think about it: Exclusiveness is a cherished characteristic of all religious groups. Orthodox Jews don't want to be required to give up their dietary laws; Quakers don't want to be forced to serve in the military; fundamentalist Christians don't want evolution to be taught to their children. If you want to teach evolution, don't expect fundamentalists to accept you as a Sunday school teacher. Likewise, don't eat non-kosher food and expect to be counted an

Orthodox Jew. Since the time of Abraham, adhering to a belief system is what religion is all about. "When in Rome ..." as the saying goes.

In the church, we often expect people to do what the Romans do, but we also recognize that Rome can change — and that brings controversies anew. My own denomination, the Presbyterian Church (USA), lost congregations a generation ago when it decided to break with tradition and insist on the ordination of women. This was a Moses-style exodus from a long history of women being barred from ordained leadership. While some Presbyterians argued for excluding women from leadership on the grounds of traditional understandings of scripture, others pushed for acceptance based on a modern belief in divine inclusiveness — the notion that God desires the inclusion of all people, which is suggested by scripture such as the passage displayed in the sanctuary of Fairfax Presbyterian Church: "A House of Prayer for All Peoples." Given the gifts of ministry that my female colleagues clearly have, I am glad that the inclusive forces won that debate.

The drive toward inclusiveness is motivating the National Cathedral in Washington — long associated with the Episcopal Church — to increase its outreach to the community and make its ministry more interdenominational. "We acknowledge who we are — an Episcopal cathedral," says Robert Becker of the Office of Program and Pastoral Ministries. "But we also stress the fact that this cathedral is indeed a house of prayer for all people. Often, that translates into special interfaith services that are held here." In 2001, there was a dedication of the final stained glass window in the cathedral, one that recalls the hope of the Hebrew people to return to Jerusalem after exile in Babylon. Invited participants included notable Jewish figures such as Supreme Court Justice Ruth Bader Ginsberg and Rabbi Irving Greenberg, chairman of the United States Holocaust Memorial Council.

But how "interfaith" can an Episcopal cathedral be, given the centrality of Jesus in the building's liturgy, art, and architecture? That's a question that no book can answer; it must be worked out in the experience of the community. Michael Wyatt, director of religious education, told me that " 'A house of prayer for all people' does not mean to me that all individuals would find here — or are even entitled to find here — a service that they would have designed on their own. The ownership of ritual prayer is not individualistic." While the cathedral offers a genuine welcome to every guest, its hospitality is grounded in a distinctively Christian tradition. Liberation and obligation have to remain in a kind of creative tension, as the virtue of inclusiveness is balanced with the virtue of exclusiveness.

Indeed, my friend, Timothy Merrill, senior editor of the preaching journal *Homiletics*, doesn't think that it is possible to provide a worship style that appeals to everyone. "What you find in the middle of the road is usually dead, road-kill worship that leaves a bad taste in the mouth for everyone." He argues that there is "a strong movement that leaps back ... to medieval expressions of piety, such as chants, prayers, and plainsong" — traditions that he senses provide more opportunities for theological reflection than contemporary worship styles.

But what if people are uncomfortable with medieval chants, and are looking for a more "user-friendly," contemporary worship experience? "We live in an 'experience' economy," observes Phil Beauchene, an elder at Fairfax Presbyterian Church, reminding me that "Disney doesn't sell you a ride, it sells you an experience." He is convinced that we could use drama and multimedia to better advantage in worship, and I think he's right — we should be liberated from traditional styles of preaching and praying. What he's talking about, of course, is changing the way we deliver the message, not changing the message itself.

But sometimes our effort to reach people runs the risk of diluting or altering that message. That's a key issue for Phil and his wife, Carolyn Klein, who is heavily involved in ministries of music and Christian education at Fairfax: Should Fairfax have different types of services to appeal to specific groups? Should the church offer a contemporary service on Saturday evening for those who are on the periphery of organized religion — a kind of "lite church" that could draw people in? Carolyn and Phil worry that if the church works too hard at being acceptable to everyone, it will end up not standing for anything in particular. There is no virtue in throwing out our core beliefs and obligations in the quest for complete inclusiveness.

So, how did I resolve the issue of the memorial service involving church outsiders? My friend and I settled on a passage of scripture in which Elisha asks his departing mentor Elijah for "a double share of your spirit" (2 Kings 2:9) — a passage that is well-grounded in the Bible, but also accessible to a gathering of nonreligious people. In other words, I invited them to Rome, without expecting them to speak Italian immediately.

Such attempts to transmit the tradition, and to train a new generation of Christians in virtuous behavior, will become increasingly important in our multicultural and religiously pluralistic world. In the end, the challenge that religious communities face is not to be relevant, but to be clear — about their beliefs, their practices, their scriptures, their morals, their outreach projects, their organizational structures. "From the beginning, Christians have said that what is relevant *is* the tradition," observes Wyatt of the National Cathedral. If the church does not have a distinctive message to offer society, then it has ceased to be a true religious voice. It has become just another cultural phenomenon, one that will quickly be replaced by the next spiritual fad.

That sort of focus on tradition will inevitably lead to the kind of conflict represented by the Salvation Army's response to homosexual activity. Sometimes the church will embark on an exodus and change, as my denomination did over the ordination of women; sometimes it will keep the covenant and stick with tradition, as the Salvation Army is insisting it will. That may lead the organization to back away from federal funding and concentrate on its own community of faith — which is not a bad thing.

Such an approach serves as a reminder that most people come to church in search of a distinctive and recognizable "house of prayer" — an organization that is open to all, but not one that is trying to be all things to all people. That means that pastors like me have to be prepared to make a stand once in a while for things that will be unacceptable to others. We will do this not because moral clarity is always superior to Christian charity, but because both clarity and charity are interlocking virtues in our practice of the faith. On a practical level, this means that we have to focus on being clear, not relevant — clear about our beliefs, our scriptures, our morals, and our mission projects.

As we live out the faith in community — remembering that virtuous living is a team sport, not an individual activity — we discover that the perspectives of Abraham and Moses both have important roles to play, and that their contributions of obligation, liberation, exclusiveness, and inclusiveness can all be used for the good, if kept in the proper balance. In the ongoing life of the church, this can be done by making an effort to match young people with adult role models, in tutoring programs, confirmation classes, fellowship events, and mission projects. It can be accomplished by taking the time in worship to celebrate personal milestones, such as fiftieth wedding anniversaries, moments that capture important images of moral clarity and Christian charity. Together, Moses and Abraham can guide us as we attempt to develop true Christian character — not only for our own benefit, but for the good of the next generation of Christians, and all who enter our houses of prayer.

Chapter Seven

The People And The Pope

It's October 1995. Pope John Paul II travels through the streets of Baltimore in a papal parade, celebrates Mass at the Camden Yards baseball stadium, and is cheered by a multitude of Roman Catholics. He is their leader, their role model, their Holy Father — the one they believe to be God's deputy, the Vicar of Christ. They understand that he speaks for the Catholics of the world, and they appreciate his messages of moral clarity in a relativistic world.

Joining these Catholics, in spirit if not in person, are many Protestants who secretly wish they had a pope. Despite the fact that their churches were formed by Christians desperate to escape papal authority, these Protestants admire John Paul II and many dimensions of his leadership of the Catholic Church. If their own denominations could work out the organizational details, they would really like a pope of their own. Why is this?

For starters, the pope is a symbol of the unity of the Catholic Church. While it is said that Baptists "multiply by division," forming new congregations every time a church splits, Catholics remain united under the leadership of the Bishop of Rome. This is not to say that all Catholics agree with the pope's teachings — in fact, a majority of American Catholics, according to a 2003 *Washington Post-ABC News* poll, dissent from the pope's teachings on birth control, premarital sex, and the death penalty. But all do have a connection to the same Holy Father, and eighty percent approve of the way the pope has done his job. Although they are not "one big happy family" — especially in the wake of recent clergy sexual-abuse scandals — Catholics are clearly a family, Baltimore to Bangkok.

"The Bishop of Rome does offer an important sign for the unity of the church," notes the Reverend Dr. L. Gregory Jones. This United

Methodist minister was, at the time of the pope's visit, an associate professor of theology at Loyola College in Baltimore. "He reminds Protestants of the scandal of disunity. The pope seeks reconciliation among the churches, most recently in his encyclical titled, 'That All May Be One.'"

I am also impressed by the fact that the pope speaks with remarkable clarity. Whether you agree with him or not, you have to admit that John Paul II has a strong sense of covenant, and he is completely clear about where he stands. Pro-life. Pro-celibate-priesthood. Anti-contraception. Anti-ordination-of-women. Ninety percent of American Catholics feel that the pope has done a good-to-excellent job of setting a personal moral example, and even non-Christians admire him for holding on to strong beliefs in our morally wavering world.

Protestants tired of the diversity of stands in their own churches, where "individual conscience" rules, are drawn to the clarity of the pope's positions. They may not always like what he says, but at least they know what he is saying. "I think he has stood up for a lot of things," said Bob Maifarth, a Florida Presbyterian, to *The Washington Post* in October 2003, "saying that just because it's the year 2000-and-something, that doesn't mean what's in the Bible has to change."

Some Protestants "are looking for someone to speak with pastoral authority in our time," reflects the Reverend Dr. Edward W. Castner, former Associate General Presbyter of National Capital Presbytery. They are asking: "Where are the standards for today? Who is speaking out for them?" Instead of a pope, Presbyterians have a denominational headquarters that does not, according to Castner, "seem like a place of authority, tradition, and pastoral concern. It is more of an administrative functioning unit."

John Paul II is "remarkably thoughtful and profound," adds Jones, and the pope shows signs of being a fan of the exodus, working for the liberation of the oppressed. "This pope offers a sign of hope to a fragmented and despairing world. He has been critical of consumerism and materialism, and knows what the culture of death looks like. The pope's theological passion and exemplary witness shine through the darkness of disbelief, bureaucracy, and chaos."

In addition, the pope is a leader with a human touch. I was once given a humorous coffee mug which defines Protestantism in the following way: "It's the thought that counts." (The same mug's definition of Catholicism: "Stop thinking those thoughts.") Focus on "thought" is a problem for Protestantism, because Christianity has always been a very earthy religion. Jesus: God in human flesh. Communion: The body and the blood. Church: The body of Christ. While some may say, "The pope is only a man," others will say, "Exactly. That's the point." The pope is a human, representing God-in-human-form. There is power in his flesh-and-blood presence, in his ability to speak with visitors in their own languages, in his human touch.

For all of these reasons, I knew that there would be little protest from Protestants when the pope visited Baltimore in 1995. But just a few years later, parishioners in the Roman Catholic Church began to express intense dissatisfaction with the way in which their church hierarchy was handling cases of sexual abuse by Catholic clergy, culminating in a 2003 *Washington Post-ABC News* poll finding that 74 percent of American Catholics believed that the pope should have done more to address the problem of sexual abuse of children and teenagers by priests. One group in particular, "Voice of the Faithful," rose up from the grass roots in early 2002 and began to talk about making the Catholic Church more democratic, with the goal of gaining more governing rights for the laity. The faithful parishioners who had always looked up to the pope were now asking for the pope to become more accountable to the people.

When Voice of the Faithful gathered several thousand Catholics in Boston in July 2002, I understood both the depth of their concern and the direction they wanted to go. Rallying around the motto "Keep the Faith, Change the Church," they were riding a wave of outrage over the clergy sexual-abuse crisis, and they wanted to shift power downward from the top of their hierarchical church. In a little over six months, Voice of the Faithful had grown to 16,000 members from forty states and 21 countries, and was well on its way to becoming a force to be reckoned with in the governing bodies of the Roman Catholic Church.

As a Presbyterian pastor, committed to democratic church government, my initial reaction was simply to say, "Welcome to my world." I spend every day serving an institution that puts power in the hands of laypeople — and I'm well aware of the assets and liabilities of such an approach. While having a voice and a vote certainly gives people more opportunities for institutional involvement and may even inspire greater commitment to the church's benevolent works, the process of democratization can also dilute the purity of the church's moral message and undermine its influence in larger political and social spheres. Furthermore, I am aware of no hard evidence that lay leadership provides protection against church scandals — which is what many Voice of the Faithful members seem to be hoping. We Presbyterians know that there is no panacea to be found in shifting power from the pope to the people.

It is important to keep in mind that one of the great strengths of the Catholic Church has been the influence it derives from the unity of its message at every level of church life. From solid grass-roots support for its parochial school system to the commitment to Third World debt relief exemplified by Pope John Paul II's underwriting of the Jubilee 2000 debt-relief campaign, Catholicism has a social and political impact few other religions can imagine. Catholics have been able to do the work of Christian charity largely because they have practiced moral clarity.

In contrast are Protestant Christians such as the Presbyterians, a group with a very different history and philosophy. My current congregation, Fairfax Presbyterian, like any other Presbyterian church, is a representative democracy. As I explain to new members of my church, Presbyterians are ruled by "presbyters" — the Greek word for "elders" — and decisions about the life and ministry of the church are made primarily by laypeople elected and ordained to serve as those elders. The result is that on some issues — and particularly politically charged ones such as abortion or the ordination of gays and lesbians — the Presbyterian Church speaks with many voices, revising its policies over time and sometimes changing direction altogether.

That is contrary to traditional Catholic practice. "The idea that any board in a diocese could have independence from the authority of the bishop of the diocese is utterly *non*-Catholic," observes my friend Bill Parent, a priest in the Archdiocese of Washington, "something akin to disgruntled Presbyterians clamoring for a pope." While he's all in favor of laypeople serving on church boards, he reminds me that all such participation must relate to the role of the Catholic bishop as "chief shepherd" of the diocese.

But Voice of the Faithful — and about a dozen other reform groups — seems to be at the forefront of a more general change in the culture of the Catholic Church, at least in the United States. Dean Hoge, a sociologist at Catholic University, tells me that young Catholics see the teaching authority of the Vatican as much less important than do the older members of the church; in a 1999 survey, thirty percent of those born after Vatican II was introduced in the early '60s, said it is important, compared with 64 percent of the pre-Vatican II generation. And the 2003 *Washington Post-ABC News* poll revealed that 64 percent of American Catholics think that the next pope should change church policies to reflect the attitudes and lifestyles of Catholics today.

Changes are clearly underway, and while they may lead to more active involvement from people in the pews, they could also cause deterioration in church unity. Over the years, Catholics have enjoyed both institutional unity and remarkable moral clarity, and parishioners have been given a clear sense of which direction their moral guidepost points. Consider the way Catholic teaching about the sanctity of life has affected health care delivery, especially at the end of life — Catholic hospitals have led the way in providing palliative care for dying patients. But today there is not necessarily more of a unified "Catholic vote" than a "Protestant vote" in this country. In the 2000 presidential election, more Catholics voted for pro-choice Al Gore than for pro-life George Bush, according to exit polls.

Catholics are becoming more like Presbyterians, a group of Christians that has trouble coming to a clear national consensus about some controversial issues because there are 2.5 million of us holding 2.5 million beliefs. With regard to abortion, for example, my denomination has been basically pro-choice, although pro-life Presbyterians have pushed to modify the policy over the years. We now oppose abortion as a means of birth control and gender selection, affirm adoption as preferable to the abortion of unwanted children, and consider the "intact dilation and extraction" procedure (also called "partial birth abortion") a "matter of grave moral concern."

Is this lack of moral clarity good or bad? It depends. Whether you consider this a weak, mixed message or a realistic one that parishioners will actually follow, it serves as an excellent illustration of our democratic church government in action. Sometimes politically charged issues split us down the middle, which is what has happened over the issue of ordaining gays and lesbians. Several years ago a desire for clarity led to the introduction of a "fidelity and chastity" clause which excludes sexually active gays and lesbians from ordination. Our national General Assembly voted to remove the requirement in 2001 (Christian charity); and our regional presbyteries voted to preserve it in 2002 (moral clarity).

That's just the kind of division — healthy in some lights, destructive in others — that could come to characterize a more democratic Catholic Church, because I doubt that 63 million American Catholics are going to behave very differently from 2.5 million American Presbyterians. And while the leaders of Voice of the Faithful have announced the ambitious goal of getting half of the nation's Catholics involved, and are actively courting the broad middle of the laity, I don't know how they'll avoid the hot-button issues that tend to divide church groups. One of the founders of Voice of the Faithful, Svea Fraser, tells me that they're not taking on those issues now, although they know that they'll eventually come up. "All we want now," she says, "is to find a place at the table, where all voices can be heard." But all those voices are sure to express a huge variety of opinions.

While I have concerns about democratic forms of church government, I'm not opposed to them — I wouldn't be a Presbyterian pastor if I were. In fact, I believe that being liberated from hierarchical control frees us to be energetic followers of Moses, and to do the work of Christian charity with personal passion. In my experience, there is nothing more powerful than a group of people who feel called by God to perform a particular mission, whether it be serving on a church board, teaching a class, repairing the home of a low-income neighbor, or starting a new church. And in terms of Sunday offerings, which are one important measure of commitment, studies have shown that Protestants give higher portions of their income to the work of the church — often two or three times greater — than Catholics.

When my associate pastor and I meet with our elders for our monthly board meetings, I am often amazed by the skills and insights that these sixteen laypeople bring to the work of Fairfax Presbyterian Church. As a group of men and women, young and old, liberal and conservative, married and single, with careers ranging from academics to engineering to national security, we represent the broader congregation — and whenever we face a challenging issue together, I have been consistently grateful for the clear guidance of these elders.

There are fewer places to hide in a church that depends on such lay leadership, and fewer ways to remain passive. In theory, if not always in practice, the unique set of insights, talents, and energy of every church member is needed to make a democratic congregation work. When functioning properly, such a church feels more like a religious movement than a religious institution, and it leans closer to the exodus of Moses than to the covenant of Abraham.

Some Catholics seem ready for this sort of democratic decision making. Lena Woltering, the coordinator of a lay group called FOSIL — Fellowship of Southern Illinois Laity — tells me that in their vision of church reform, "the model of shared authority and ownership is certainly something we are working toward." If this goal is achieved, it will transform the church no less profoundly than did the Protestant Reformation of the sixteenth century. Others, however, resist the notion of change. Susan Gibbs, spokeswoman for the Catholic Archdiocese of Washington, observes that most reform groups are small, recalling that in the late '90s, a group called "We Are Church" announced they would gather one million signatures from American Catholics in one year to support a number of reforms. "After extending their deadline an extra six months, they barely hit 30,000, if that," Gibbs told me in 2002.

Whatever the fate of the new reform movements, there will always be some who feel drawn to the clarity of Catholicism, and other Christians who seek the Protestant process of continual consensus building. The practical challenge for Catholics — and other Christians with hierarchical forms of church government — is to find ways to allow parishioners to take a role in shaping the mission and ministry of the church. The opposite challenge, for Presbyterians and others with democratic forms of church government, is to work on achieving consensus among church members, and speaking with moral clarity about issues of concern.

Still, within every community of faith, there will be not only a longing for an Abrahamic pope, but also a hunger to be liberated, Moses-style, from captivity to a church hierarchy. Both desires can be beneficial to society, but in widely divergent ways, with Catholic unity providing spiritual and social stability and Protestant diversity offering ever-changing religious and communal opportunities. It takes all sorts, I know, and I have to trust that God is present in not only the obligations and moral clarity being lifted up by Catholics, but also in the work of liberation and Christian charity being done by Protestants. The challenge for church leaders is to keep these qualities in a state of creative tension, never allowing one to completely dominate the life of the Christian community.

Chapter Eight

Clarity Versus Charity

As a parish pastor, I often find myself acting as a sort of go-between. I'm both mouthpiece of a national denomination and spokesman for the members of my own church. I try to provide guidance according to the individual needs and situations of my parishioners, and also to follow the lead given by the Presbyterian Church (USA). None of the issues I wrestle with — from race relations to evangelism to abortion — presents me and my congregation with a trickier stumbling block than that of the role that gays and lesbians play in the church.

It's a stumbling block because in the church we are forced to live with complex questions that the larger community often brushes aside or ignores entirely. Many people have deep, unspoken feelings about homosexuality, but they are afraid to publicly condemn or condone it. In the church — an institution that people look to for moral guidance — we cannot take such evasive action.

The issue of homosexuality was highlighted for me in 1999 as I followed news of the General Assembly of the Presbyterian Church, meeting in Fort Worth, Texas. Commissioners once again debated a question that had raised passions and anxieties within the denomination for more than twenty years: Whether to ordain gays and lesbians who are open about their sexual orientation. A 1978 General Assembly policy prohibits the ordination of "self-affirming, practicing homosexuals."

In an effort to chip away at that policy, an assembly committee had recommended deleting a constitutional requirement that deacons, elders, and ministers live either in "fidelity within the covenant of marriage between a man and a woman, or [in] chastity in singleness." This committee was doing the work of liberation and attempting to show Christian charity toward gays and lesbians who feel called to serve as leaders of the church. But, at the end of the meeting, the General Assembly as a whole rejected this recommendation, preserving the status quo — the Assembly asserted traditional obligations and took a stand for moral clarity. More often than not, debates about the role of homosexuals in the church boil down to this struggle between charity and clarity.

Perhaps it was inevitable that the debate in 1999 seemed to hinge on extreme positions. At the meeting, a lesbian activist named Janie Spahr argued that the denomination's stringent policies have been "killing lesbian, gay, bisexual, and transgendered people. The church is participating in our deaths." Her words were heartfelt and passionate, but seemed to me to be an overstatement of her case. At the other end of the spectrum, Julius Poppinga, an elder from New Jersey, said, "Repentance is the key" — in other words, repentance of any practice that scripture and the standards of the church call sin. But this, too, is an extreme position, and is far more easily said than done. There are many biblical prohibitions, not all of which we follow to the letter, from lending money with interest to the poor of God's people (Exodus 22:25) and the mixing of different materials in clothing (Leviticus 19:19), to the starkly clear "root of all evil": the love of money (1 Timothy 6:10). Why do we put such emphasis on the handful of verses that declare homosexual activity a sin, such as "You shall not lie with a male as with a woman"? (Leviticus 18:22).

All of which leaves me wondering: What am I to do when I preach a Sunday sermon, or try to offer guidance to members of the congregation who are wrestling with these questions in their personal lives? I'm all for fidelity and chastity — fundamental Christian values that I try to practice and preach — but I can't help but feel that the debate over homosexuality continues to reveal a disconnect between the General Assembly and the congregations it represents. The 1999 debate did represent some shift in attitude — and a split in church leadership — but it was not very enlightening to gays and straights who would rather serve the church — and God — together than sit in judgment of each other. If denominational pronouncements are missing the mark with Presbyterians, then they are surely way off course with the community at large.

I don't mean to deny the importance of the ordination issue for my congregation. Far from it. The question of what role gays and lesbians should play vexes many Presbyterians, probably many more than will openly voice their views. The voices I hear in my congregation are occasionally strident — one couple left Calvary Presbyterian after I preached a sermon suggesting that because companionship is part of God's plan for us, it may be possible for homosexuals to live in faithful, monogamous relationships. On the other extreme, another couple joined a more liberal denomination in another state after forty years in the Presbyterian Church because they were tired of the homosexual issue being "continually swept under the rug, or referred back to a committee for more study." But far more often I hear parishioners saying that they want to be a friendly and welcoming church, and to be a support to fellow Christians regardless of their sexual orientation. When a person is discovered to be gay or lesbian, church members tend to be more interested in his or her peace of mind than in his or her sex life. Christian charity seems to be the default position of most Presbyterians, regardless of how they rank homosexual activity in terms of moral clarity.

One elder at Calvary, a true pillar of the congregation, spoke openly about her opposition to homosexuality, based on her experience of having a close friend with a gay son. She couldn't and wouldn't support his homosexual behavior, she told our board of elders, and yet she acknowledged that this son was the only child in the family who took care of his mother. Her mixed opinion of him was clearly based on more than his sexuality, and it created in her a tension between disgust and admiration that I see in many straight people's views of individual gays and lesbians. They intuitively sense that it is wrong to judge a whole person based solely on sexual orientation, and so they refrain from condemnation in the community and in the church.

This same kind of broad-based assessment is made whenever my church — first Calvary, and now Fairfax — nominates and elects people to serve as church officers. To my knowledge, no candidates are ever asked point-blank about fidelity, chastity, or sexual orientation, but instead are evaluated on the strength of their beliefs and their gifts for church leadership. Christian virtues such as faithfulness, commitment, love, and sacrifice are seen as central to fitness for ministry. While this may not make us the most rule-abiding of Presbyterians, I frankly don't know of any other way to select church leaders.

The congregations I have served see what the national Presbyterian leaders cannot — namely, how people behave in a particular community of faith, where it doesn't take long to figure out whether a person is reckless or promiscuous or abusive or unloving. Of course, if an elder were to make a public spectacle of his sexuality — whether heterosexual or homosexual — I believe that his days in leadership would be numbered. Although my parishioners have been charitable toward gays and lesbians, this does not mean that they lack moral clarity about what constitutes proper Christian conduct in the community. They know that sexual behavior must always be taken very seriously, and both congregations have taken steps to protect children, in particular, from sexual predators.

So, how do we know where to stand as liberation-seekers ... and obligation-keepers? Do we place our primary emphasis on Christian charity or on moral clarity? For now, the law of the Presbyterian land remains fidelity and chastity. This pleases my conservative church members, including those who follow scripture's condemnation of homosexual practice and say quite simply, "It is an abomination." But it disturbs my more liberal members, who see this as a justice issue, and want the Presbyterian Church to be more welcoming toward gays and lesbians, as Jesus was toward the outcasts of his day.

Once again, I find myself acting as a go-between — not always able to mediate between such differing points of view, or to give people an unambiguous "word of the Lord." If I were asked to take a stand for moral clarity and enforce the fidelity and chastity regulation, my first question would have to be: How? By employing private detectives? Public whistle-blowing? Periodic examinations? I'm not quite sure how to regulate covenant-keeping when the area of concern is the most intimate details of a person's sex life.

It is better, I think, to move in a charitable direction and call people to do their best to be faithful in all their relationships, trusting all the while that the community will know goodness when it sees it. My guess is that we are moving toward a new place in which faithful, committed, monogamous relationships among homosexuals will become acceptable in the Christian community; after all, who would have guessed just a few centuries ago that churches would defy tradition by helping to free slaves and work for the equality of women? The church is in the business of encouraging promise-keeping, self-control, and steadfast love — goals that should be encouraged in all communities and among gays as well as straights. This is the kind of moral clarity that even the most passionate liberation-seeker can embrace.

Of course, we have not completed this exodus and made it into the promised land. One of the biggest obstacles we face is the growth of litigation in Protestant denominations — the use of formal trials in the courts of the church to resolve issues such as the ordination of gays and lesbians, and same-sex marriage. Across the ecumenical landscape, clergy and other church leaders are finding themselves in ecclesiastical courts over questions of theology and issues involving sexuality, and many are facing a charge one might have thought had gone out with witch burnings: heresy.

Yes, heresy trials are making a comeback, affecting congregations and lives in profound ways. Examples abound: An elder in the Orthodox Presbyterian Church lost his position after teaching evolution at a Michigan college. A Lutheran pastor from Brooklyn faced heresy charges for consorting with "pagans" after taking part in an interfaith gathering with Muslims, Sikhs, and Hindus at Yankee Stadium in New York after September 11, 2001. A Methodist minister in Omaha, charged for performing gay marriages, was convicted by a church tribunal and relieved of his ministerial credentials. The Methodist bishop of Chicago was recently cleared of heresy for saying he did not believe that the resurrection involved the resuscitation of Jesus' physical body. And in the Presbyterian Church (USA), the Reverend Stephen Van Kuiken of Cincinnati, who was accused of heresy and blasphemy for marrying same-sex

97

couples in violation of church law, was removed from the ministry on June 16, 2003.

At the time of Van Kuiken's removal, there were more than 25 disciplinary cases pending in the Presbyterian Church alone, many more than we had seen at one time since the 1920s. You had to wonder what was behind this sudden rash of litigation. "In some respects, [it] reflects our society's common resort to formal litigation as a grievance process," observed Craig M. McKee, a Terre Haute, Indiana, attorney and my fellow trustee in the National Cathedral Association. "A lawsuit is increasingly the way we communicate to others that 'we mean business.'"

Yet at bottom, all of these cases, whether they arise over Christology or sexuality, reveal an ongoing, and growing, tension — the tension between diversity and purity. Proponents of diversity want to accept a broader range of sexual orientations and theological perspectives, while believers in purity want to enforce traditional morality and theological clarity. This is yet another manifestation of the obligation-liberation struggle, with covenant-keepers fighting for purity and clarity, and exodus-seekers pushing for diversity and charity.

Such tensions are tricky because they don't break down clearly into right and wrong, or good versus evil. As I look over my congregation in Fairfax, I realize that this diversity-purity dichotomy is a balancing act, one that is constantly being performed by church members and myself. Part of my job as a pastor is to be open to new understandings of sexuality and theology, and to share these developments with my congregation, but at the same time I am charged with being a guardian of traditional truths and a dispenser of clear guidance. It is difficult for me to know how much to preserve and how much to change. I want the church to be a strong supporter of traditional marriage, for instance, but I also want it to make room for gays and lesbians who feel anguish because their monogamous relationships are not recognized. At times I feel as though these heresy trials, especially those centered on homosexuality, are being staged not only within the courts of the church, but also within myself.

"There is no doubt that the U.S. is undergoing cultural change," says Dean Hoge, a professor of sociology at Catholic University. He points to rapid immigration, growing pluralism, new sensitivities about ecumenism (especially since 9/11), and ever-increasing acceptance of homosexuality — of which the Supreme Court's ruling in 2003, overturning Texas' ban on sodomy, is being seen as just the latest manifestation. Hoge does not find it surprising that church members take opposing positions on the problems created by such change, but he believes, as a Presbyterian, that the best way for faithful Protestants to find their way is "through deliberation, debate, and votes of national groups, not through the courts."

Using church courts to adjudicate these matters is certainly expensive and time-consuming. Church consultant and Episcopal priest Loren Mead has seen again and again "how debilitating to presbyteries and other judicatories are the interminable legal hassles." At present, the Presbyterian Church (USA) is being forced to respond to allegations filed by a single individual, a Reston, Virginia, attorney named Paul Jensen, who is responsible for a majority of the current cases in the denomination. He is demanding that presbyteries across the country discipline more than twenty ministers who have allegedly disobeyed church law. The first of these cases to go to trial was Reverend Van Kuiken's. The blow his removal has inflicted on him and his congregation is a stark reminder of how high the stakes are in each of these cases. A married man with children, Van Kuiken has now lost his job. Should he ever want to be a Presbyterian minister again, he would have to go through the ordination process from scratch. Still, he remains convinced that the issue of same-sex marriages is not going to go away.

It is certainly the right of every church to enforce its laws and require that its clergy conform to certain doctrines. Attorney McKee argues that denominations or churches with a judicial process in place, whatever its nature, must respect that structure. "It would be misguided and wrong to abolish or limit those processes to avoid controversy," he says, for peace does not come through putting limitations on the grievance process. He predicted that the Episcopal Church could "find itself in the throes of a painful, bitter, even embarrassing debate" when its General Convention met in 2003 to decide whether or not to approve the election of a gay bishop by the diocese of New Hampshire — but he was confident that it would conduct the debate in the context of its code of laws.

The basic problem with law enforcement in the Christian Church is that Jesus Christ himself was no legalist. He frequently performed the work of liberation and broke established purity laws to minister to outcasts in his own society. Pastors like Van Kuiken argue that they are being faithful to Jesus when they break with tradition to marry gays and lesbians, and in many cases they have the full support of their congregations. Van Kuiken's 280-member Mount Auburn Presbyterian Church is about one-third gay, and it has long been committed to the full participation of homosexuals. While Paul Jensen certainly had a legal right to file an allegation against Van Kuiken, his complaint was not grounded in the convictions or experiences of Van Kuiken's Cincinnati congregation.

There is also the question of how best to define purity in a religious tradition that is constantly reforming itself. Susan Andrews, the pastor of Bradley Hills Presbyterian Church in Bethesda, Maryland, observes that over the course of biblical history, the understanding of religious purity has changed. For example, the prophet Isaiah contradicts the purity codes of Leviticus and Deuteronomy by including in the religious community two categories of people who had been excluded before — "foreigners" and "eunuchs" (Isaiah 56:1-8). Those who had once been excluded on ritual grounds are now included because they honor God in their actions and relationships. "I believe that our purity battles today do not adequately reflect the unfolding notion of purity in scripture," Andrews says. "A purity of law turns into a purity of love, embodied in the gracious and hospitable ministry of Jesus Christ."

So the tension being felt by Christians today is not simply a pull between diversity and purity — it is also a tug between different definitions of purity. It is my belief that we will eventually move beyond the notion that only heterosexuals can practice moral purity in their sexual relationships, and we will come to see that promise-keeping, self-control, and steadfast love can be practiced by gays as well as straights. The traditional obligation to practice sexuality only within heterosexual marriage will be replaced by a new obligation to be faithful in a promise-based, monogamous relationship, whether gay or straight. We will reach this new understanding by being willing to walk the path of liberation, but also by continuing to debate the merits of charity and clarity, diversity and purity.

Of course, such debates are anything but new. My colleague, Fred Lyon, interim pastor of Brown Memorial Park Avenue Presbyterian Church in Baltimore, claims that "heretics, not infrequently, are prophets ahead of our clarification curve." Looking back on recent "heresies" such as the ordination of women and divorced people, he sees that progress occurred precisely because heretics forced us to clarify our faith. The root of the word "heresy" is a Greek word meaning "to choose," which is, of course, what religious people are challenged to do in any era.

Still, I wish this process of choosing and clarifying could go on primarily in local congregations, instead of the courts of the church. On a practical level, these issues are much better handled through deliberation and debate on the local level, not by legal actions in the courts of the church. If these matters continue to be taken to court, I fear that our churches will lose their attractiveness to a new generation. In my congregation, I see young people drawn by lively worship services, thoughtful discussions, and opportunities to engage in exciting mission projects, and at the same time becoming confused and disenchanted by church fights. People can be well served by genuine debate about what Christ's teachings mean and how to apply them, says McKee, but if Christians take actions designed to exclude and punish, "the church will be viewed by an already skeptical world as cruel, hypocritical, and irrelevant."

After all, people come to church to find a community of love, spiritual growth, and sacrificial service, not a stained-glass version of our litigious secular world. They enter our doors to find both purity and diversity — not groups of people who are constantly at war over what constitutes the most Christ-centered and virtuous life. Most of all, they come to church to encounter a God who has created both gays and straights, and to find the help they need in order to act with love and faithfulness in committed, monogamous relationships, regardless of sexual orientation.

101

To help people achieve these goals, church leaders need to perform a balancing act between Christian charity and moral clarity, following the very best guidance of spiritual leaders such as Moses and Abraham. This means making a broad-based assessment of those who feel called to serve the church, focusing on their beliefs, their behaviors, and their spiritual gifts — not just their sexual orientations. It also means challenging everyone to be faithful in all of their relationships, trusting the community to know goodness when it sees it. It is only when we have faith in God and in each other that we will discover the path that lies ahead — a path that will surely be marked by both moral clarity and Christian charity.

Chapter Nine

The Young Have Faith In Action

Everywhere you look, people are focusing on faith and searching for meaning in life. Americans attend church far more often than the residents of other industrialized countries. Ninety-four percent of us, when asked, say we are religious. Angels are popular on television, and books for the soul are bestsellers. *The Purpose-Driven Life*, a book by California minister Rick Warren, sold over eleven million copies in 2003 alone.

You might assume that all of this would have the effect of making it easier to write a Sunday sermon. Instead, the widening gulf in my parishioners' approaches to religion makes reaching them harder than ever. When my messages focus on the great doctrines of Christianity — salvation, grace, and faith — I know that I am speaking the language of the seniors of my church, the Abrahamic language of covenant-keeping. But those words mean little to many of their fellow pew sitters — particularly teenagers and young adults who are looking to go in a new direction.

There's more to this issue than rhetorical strategies. I know that my ability — or inability — to reach the younger generation has profound consequences for the future of the church. Sure, I need to preach solid Christian doctrine and satisfy the older folks who fill most of the church's pews and offering plates. But I am also called to speak of our faith using modern images and contemporary cultural references, in an attempt to reach a generation that finds meaning in movies, popular music, online chatting, and — increasingly — altruistic action. If I ignore this perspective, I'm afraid I will put the health and future of my church in peril.

Many mainline denominations — including my own, the Presbyterian Church (USA) — have done a terrible job of reaching the younger generation. We are a graying church: More than half of all members of my denomination are older than fifty, and one-third are 65 or older. A good part of our staggering membership losses since the 1960s can be attributed to our failure to keep our children in church and attract other young people. And I think that may be because we're going about trying to attract them in the wrong way. Young people like to be where the action is. Although they may not be able to recite the biblical story of Moses, they instinctively want to follow him on a journey to a promised land.

Just look at the widespread popularity of summer youth mission projects. This is kind of a "stealth" movement — not reported in the news media the way youth abstinence movements and school prayer efforts have been — but it is revitalizing youth groups across the country. Teenagers spend a week in the summer building houses in Mexico, working with children in West Virginia, or cleaning up flood damage in North Carolina — focusing more on Christian action than on Christian doctrine. Since the mid-1990s, youth groups from my congregations have been going on mission trips every summer, and enthusiasm has been very high.

This may be a key to the renewal of graying congregations and a benefit to a larger society that is looking for committed people to pick up some of the social service work once provided by government. It harks back to the earliest church, which attracted members not through "right thinking" but through loving actions. People did not first understand the faith and then decide to become Christian converts; instead, notes one of my divinity school professors, George Lindbeck, "They were first attracted by the Christian community and form of life." They were attracted first by Christian charity, not by moral clarity.

They still are. "For me, Christian action is more interesting, because I would rather be involved and doing something instead of sitting and reading," said Danny Hamlin, sixteen, a student at Fairfax County's Hayfield High School, in the spring of 2000. "I get enough of that in school." Hamlin attended Calvary's mission trip to Wheeling, West Virginia, in 1999, and says he was impressed by how much respect the poor have for other people, while at the same time "they seem to get very little respect from others." His fellow mission tripper Karen Nix, a freshman at a Florida college, was struck by the number of children living in run-down neighborhoods who were "great children, but with not a lot of role models in their lives." She found it rewarding to be able to be with them for a week and show them "that people do care about them."

Teenagers are "great at seeing needs around them, and excited to do something that concretely meets the needs they see," observes Anne Marie Earley of YouthWorks! Inc., a Minneapolis-based youth mission organization with 31 mission sites in the United States, Mexico, and Canada. They are concerned about the shape of their society, and are attracted to what contemporary Jesus scholar Marcus Borg calls "a politics of compassion," instead of being drawn to "a politics of purity."

Here again, I'm seeing a strong distinction between Christian action and Christian doctrine, a distinction between liberation and obligation, if you will — one that seems to break roughly along generational lines. "Younger people don't think they need grace or salvation," a Lutheran bishop quipped at a Lenten gathering in Alexandria, Virginia, "except from credit cards!"

Many young people today — ninety percent of whom say they are "deeply spiritual," according to two recent books — are looking for something else. "I started going to church, not because I felt a need for salvation — I don't know if I even knew of the concept," reflected Robin Lyon, a senior at West Potomac High School in Fairfax County, Virginia, in the year 2000. She began attending Calvary when she was ten, even though her parents are not churchgoers. "I felt the need for meaning, and thought Christianity might be a way to find it." Lyon subsequently picked up a good bit of doctrine by attending confirmation class, joining the church, and becoming active in Sunday school, worship, and youth group — but her spiritual quest is still for meaning in life. She's on a journey, like Moses heading toward the promised land.

Another generational distinction is between older folks who identify themselves as "Presbyterian" and younger people who think of themselves as "followers of Christ." I must be an old-timer — I'm over forty — because I do have a strong personal commitment to the doctrine and organizational structure of the Presbyterian Church. But I hear younger folks — even as old as thirty — consistently identify themselves as Christians first. Ralph Paul, who was one of Calvary's leaders at age thirty, acknowledged to me, "although I have been a Presbyterian all my life and am very comfortable with the denomination, I do not feel a particularly strong tie to it." He was one of our most devoted members — an adviser to our youth group, organizer of several mission trips, member of the choir, and leader of a church committee — but said, "I would consider other denominations, if the need arose for me to find another church."

So how do the churches respond? Over the past decade, I've noticed a number of them ditching the denominations from their names. A suburban Dallas church named "Los Colinas Baptist" changed its name to "Fellowship Church" in 1990. Its membership of mostly baby boomers and younger people grew from 150 that year to 7,300 in 1999. "Most of our church wouldn't be here today if we had Baptist in the name," pastor Ed Young told *Christianity Today* magazine. Cutting across all denominations, churches with the word "community" in their title are now the largest group of Protestant Churches in the country, including converts such as New England's oldest Southern Baptist congregation, Screven Memorial Baptist in Portsmouth, New Hampshire, which recently changed its name to Seacoast Community Church.

There's no doubt in my mind that a sense of community is what draws many young people — and some of their elders — to church, rather than a particular doctrinal stance. "The most attractive aspect of church to me is the fellowship that comes with it," Kwame Boadi, a senior at Fairfax's Thomas Jefferson High School for Science and Technology, told me in the year 2000. "Going to church — and other church activities such as youth group — gives me the opportunity to congregate with people who become somewhat of an extended family." Christian doctrine was far less important to him and his peers — in fact, he said "we can easily be turned off by an incessant insistence upon a 'right way' of doing things."

Ouch. I hope that wasn't a critique of my sermons. But Boadi's comment does point to a tension in modern church life: embracing the exodus and creating an environment for spiritual searching on the one hand, versus focusing on covenant and preserving a canon

106

of traditional truths on the other. Certainly our congregation wants to welcome everyone who is searching for God, but we would be foolishly naive to assume that every seeker is necessarily on the right path all the time. What the church is in a good position to offer is a set of time-tested guidelines for religious exploration — call them "Christian doctrine," for lack of a better term — guidelines that have proved to be dependable and helpful for hundreds of years.

As a pastor, I have a hard time figuring out how to manage this tension — sometimes issuing open-ended invitations to explore the faith, and sometimes enforcing the religious rules of the road. I think that many people are also aware of this dilemma, and for them, spiritual life has become an ongoing balance between comfort and challenge. "People in general, and probably especially young people, don't like being told what to think, or what's right and wrong," observed Lyon, the youth group member who joined Calvary without her family. "But then again, I don't think religion should be changed in order to draw people in." She may have been more comfortable with the exodus motif of the liberator Moses, but she didn't necessarily want to change the traditional covenant-keeping of Father Abraham.

My own hunch is that youth mission trips provide an opportunity for beliefs to be reinforced through actions — in a "classroom" that is adventurous enough to be attractive. Kyle Becchetti of the Center for Student Missions — which organizes urban missions and service trips in several North American cities, including Washington — tells me that "Christian action can often touch the spirit and put meat on the bones of previously learned doctrine." Participants say that God becomes real to them when they step into uncomfortable situations and perform acts of Christian service. So, even though fixing up homes in downtown Wheeling may not seem as doctrinally pure as the church camp experiences of a generation ago, there is inspiration to be found in such action-oriented work projects. For young people, in particular, it may be that obligation and liberation come together most powerfully not inside the church building at all, but instead on the front lines of a challenging and adventurous mission project.

So what are the implications of this youth movement for the larger church? In this case, young people have an important lesson to teach their elders. It is becoming increasingly clear to me that congregations need to get outside of themselves if they are going to thrive, and perhaps even simply survive. A mission-minded outward orientation, such as the one taken by young people on mission trips, is desperately needed by churches that have turned inward and focused on themselves, rather than on the community around them.

Over the course of my years in the ministry, I've become ever more aware of the huge investment of time, energy, and money that American Churches put into self-preservation. This is a form of covenant-keeping that begins with the maintenance of church buildings, of course, but extends to what I call cultural transmission — the passing of particular congregational traditions, worship styles, and administrative practices from one generation to the next. Such an inward focus can lead to a range of problems, from the perpetuation of esoteric worship services to the secretive handling of sexual abuse cases. And, most importantly, it overlooks the need to concentrate first on the concerns of the larger community.

An exodus-inspired outward orientation, on the other hand, looks first to those broader needs and elevates Christian mission above institutional maintenance. Outward-looking congregations put their energy into establishing church projects in troubled areas and turn their attention to issues such as family disintegration, illiteracy, alcoholism, domestic violence, and prostitution — areas of ministry that have an enormous and obvious public benefit.

And in an unexpected way, this outward focus has an internal advantage: It results in a more vital congregation. There's a biblical underpinning for this approach. Jesus said that those who lose their lives for his sake will actually save their lives as they discover the vitality that comes through service and sacrifice. He wasn't kidding: A community orientation not only benefits society, but makes the church more appealing. People are attracted to congregations that put faith into action and set out to make a difference in the world.

Just how important this outward focus is became clear to me in 2002 when I took a ten-day trip to Brazil for a seminar led by American missionaries and Brazilian church leaders. Brazil's multicultural society has been shaped and reshaped by a number of religious movements, as has America's. While you might not think that any other country could teach Americans about marketing, in the American Church we've got some lessons to learn. Like it or not, a major challenge for us today is to become more "customer-centered" by focusing on religious mission instead of cultural transmission.

It's not that the Brazilian Christians got it right from the start. The Portuguese — especially Jesuit missionaries — imposed Christianity on Brazil's indigenous people in one of history's greatest examples of cultural transmission, expecting the Indians to believe in Christ in the same way the Europeans did. Of course, we American Christians do the very same thing today when we expect college students to regard their faith the way their grandparents do, and when we offer services and educational opportunities that look, sound, and feel very much like church life in the '50s.

I've experienced many occasions when the American Church has concentrated more on itself than on the world around it, when it has put more energy into maintenance than into mission. At Calvary Presbyterian, some members objected to the incorporation of African music and dance into our worship after Ghanaian immigrants joined the congregation. They argued that the new practices were destroying Calvary's traditional American style. Many Ghanaians, who wanted to transmit their language and culture to their children, left to form their own church.

The problem with adhering to past practices in this covenant-keeping way is that it fails in large part to carry forward the church's mission. A focus on tradition does little "to bring good news to the poor ... release to the captives and recovery of sight to the blind" (Luke 4:18). I learned on my trip that it was only in the twentieth century, when Brazilians finally broke away from the influence of European and American missionaries, that religious mission began to overcome cultural transmission there.

Today, in the Independent Presbyterian Church of Brazil, visions for church ministry arise from the needs of the community. Members have organized soccer teams for children, held dinners for neighborhood families, and created milk programs for the poor. Since violence, poor housing, bad sanitation, and sub-standard schooling are facts of life for many Brazilians — especially in urban areas — every church is challenged to take on a social project.

There are signs that such an outward focus can be a component of vital church life in the United States, but I'd like to see many more of them. Lewis Galloway, a colleague at the Brazil seminar, told me that his church, Shandon Presbyterian in Columbia, South Carolina, has a strong mission emphasis. It includes a counseling center, a child development center that ministers to more than 300 children a day, a youth center for middle school students, a campus ministry at the University of South Carolina, overseas mission trips, and building Habitat for Humanity houses. "The mission we do continuously reinvents the church," he explains. They are on a journey of liberation, making new discoveries every day as they put their energy into acts of Christian charity.

Brazilian churches take this notion of reinvention to another level: In São Paulo, the Reverend Wanderley de Mattos and his Vida Nova (New Life) Independent Presbyterian Church have started a creative ministry for children from a nearby slum. Every Saturday morning, up to seventy neighborhood kids get together to eat breakfast, sing contemporary Christian music, and attend a Bible class — gatherings that the church hopes will liberate these at-risk children from lives of drugs and violence. For many of these kids, the church becomes a place of light and joy in a city of darkness and despair.

I've been wondering why so few American Christians reach out so extensively. The threats of drugs and violence are every bit as real here, yet few churches in the Washington area have programs designed specifically to get neighborhood children off the streets. More energy goes into serving the young people of our congregations through activities that are heavy on cultural transmission, activities designed to preserve traditional obligations: youth

110

retreats, children's choirs, family nights. While we should be practicing the politics of compassion, more often than not we engage in the politics of purity.

I'm embarrassed to say that I know of no Presbyterian congregation in the Washington area that is planning to start a church extension in a slum, as Wanderley's church is doing. My own congregation, Fairfax Presbyterian, tends to concentrate on providing financial support to various established Christian social service agencies. When it comes time to start new congregations, Americans usually focus on new church development in affluent suburbs, areas where congregations can grow in membership, succeed financially, and then pump more money into the denominational coffers. Wanderley's New Life Church, on the other hand, plans to offer social action in the slums — classes on sewing, silk-screening, painting, and cleaning, designed to help the poor develop marketable skills. Its focus is not just on the soul but on the needs of the whole person. "We can and must help the needy," explained Pastor Jango Miranda, the team coordinator of a mission project in the semi-arid Sertão region of northeastern Brazil.

What really struck me, however, was how the Brazilian focus on mission has improved the culture of the church's life. In an unexpected and wonderful way, Christian charity can have the effect of enhancing moral clarity. At a Sunday evening worship service in Natal, the church was packed and more than half the worshipers were young people (quite a contrast to a typical American Church). Young people wore T-shirts with the message *Jesus: Ele Me Faz Feliz* ("Jesus: He Makes Me Happy"), and offered rousing pieces of inspirational music, complete with choreography. A young adult praise band led the congregation in lively contemporary songs. The preacher, Sherron George, a Presbyterian (USA) mission worker, reminded the congregation that the church is the church only when it exists for others.

Clearly, the church in Brazil is succeeding where we are failing — in attracting young people, and it is doing it through mission, not cultural transmission. People are naturally going to be attracted by a missionary church — one that works from the walls

111

of the church outward, focusing on compassion instead of on purity. I am reminded, of course, that much of the success of Fairfax Presbyterian's youth program stems from its focus on adventurous mission trips for junior high through college age young people every summer. Our youth have discovered that the good life truly can be found in enthusiastic service to the community.

The practical implications for congregational life are clear. We need to make an effort to support youth mission projects that focus more on Christian action than on Christian doctrine. To reach the young adults of our communities, we have to emphasize Christian community far more than denominational identity, and to increase church vitality across the generations, our challenge is going to be to elevate religious mission above institutional maintenance. In our church budgets and program plans, it is important that we join Brazilian congregations in maintaining an outward focus, and affirming that "the church is the church only when it exists for others."

There is a great deal that we in first-world churches can learn from "two-thirds world" churches such as the Independent Presbyterian Church of Brazil. While cultural transmission will always be part of the way we communicate our religious values, this activity should never be allowed to take a back seat to a primary Christian value — service to the world around us. The future of our churches may depend on understanding what our American youth and Brazilian brothers and sisters have discovered to be true: Walking the path of Christian charity is the quickest and surest way to achieve moral clarity.

Chapter Ten

What You Lose
By Looking On Your Own

While surveys tell us that 95 percent of Americans claim to believe in God, it's no secret that church attendance has been sliding in recent years. My own denomination, the Presbyterian Church (USA), has been losing members since the '60s. And, like other branches of organized religion, we are now facing a fresh challenge: a rising tide of religious books, television shows, and internet sites that invite people to practice a kind of self-help spirituality.

This issue has taken on new urgency for me since I became pastor of Fairfax Presbyterian, a congregation of about 800 adult members, in January 2001. It's a larger church with a broader range of programs than the congregation I had served previously — Calvary Presbyterian in Alexandria — but it's no less immune to the lure of private worship.

A new job always makes you reassess. This time around, I'm aware as never before that I'm not the only spiritual guide in town. As Phyllis Tickle, who writes about religious book publishing, pointed out to me, "much of what fifty years ago went into a pastor's or priest's or rabbi's study now comes [directly] to the bookstore's shelves."

People don't need to hear my sermon to get a religious message, or attend Fairfax Presbyterian's Sunday school classes to learn about approaches to prayer. It seems to Robert McKee, an electronic engineer who has served as an elder at Fairfax, as if a great many are looking elsewhere for spirituality: "My friends at work, my neighbors ... are the ones in the bookstores searching, on the internet searching."

All very well, you might say. For many people, religion is a private matter, but this shift does more than threaten to reduce the number of faces in our pews, and dilute the sense of religious obligation that can bind together the members of a congregation. It also undermines the spirit of community that is so central to the church — one that not only benefits church members but serves the world around them. Self-help spirituality weakens not only moral clarity but also Christian charity.

In our increasingly fragmented and individualistic world, it is through the strength of community that congregations can provide soup kitchens, homeless shelters, and tutoring programs. Many of those activities are well supported at the moment, but they are far harder to organize and develop without a local institution as their focus. Francis H. Wade, senior pastor of 1,800-member St. Alban's Episcopal Church in Washington, sees the value of that support system. A number of his parishioners are involved in the Washington Interfaith Network, which pushes for housing, education, and childcare. The network "connects us across the socioeconomic barriers of the city," he points out. "No individual could do that."

At Fairfax Presbyterian, we stress the community aspect of our faith through regularly scheduled programs: two youth groups, eight choirs, fourteen Christian education classes, a preschool for 100 children, and a range of groups for men, women, young adults, and families. With the help of a small army of volunteers, as well as several full-time staff members, parishioners also come together to feed the hungry, help the homeless, and, in recent years, host Belarusian children on summer visits from their homes in Chernobyl.

Even with all this activity, our efforts to create community are sometimes undermined by competing demands on parishioners' time. "Churches are not losing people to other churches," observed my friend Kent Winters-Hazelton when he was pastor of Claremont Presbyterian Church in California in 2001. "They are losing them to the weekend." People are dropping out of Sunday church to pursue leisure activities — at arts festivals, ski resorts, and beaches — and trying to make up for that by going to bookstores and internet chat rooms. Books can be read while riding the subway; internet prayer requests can be offered at 2 a.m. Both books and internet prayer sites probably seem more accessible to shy people who might be uncomfortable asking a question in a public Bible study or raising a concern in a service of worship.

What we are up against these days is big business. Lynn Garrett, the religion editor of *Publishers Weekly*, the trade magazine of the book publishing industry, tells me that the religion category in publishing has been one of the fastest growing in the past ten years, and is currently among the top three in market share, just behind popular fiction and cooking/crafts. "Many people are pursuing a private form of spirituality," she says, "and these books are a key element."

Readers are showing steady interest in spirituality, prayer, and religious living, and a rising fascination with Buddhism, grief, and Christian fiction (the *Left Behind* series — a fictional thriller based on the Bible's book of Revelation — had sold more than twenty million copies by early 2001). The content runs the gamut, from self-centered nonsense to demanding biographical and autobiographical religious works, such as the writings of Kathleen Norris. Some bookstores even have sections called "Private Spirituality," with books ranging from the reflections of Zen masters to bestsellers such as *Conversations With God.*

Although seven in ten Americans say they can be religious without going to services, my experience is that spiritual growth requires a community of support and accountability. It is amazing to see the ways church members help each other in times of illness and loss, willingly practicing Christian charity. Visits, cards, and casseroles are common signs of concern, but many congregations go much further. Some churches are making an exceptional effort to reach beyond their traditional role. The pastor, deacon, and members of St. Anthony's Roman Catholic Church in Washington care for the dying in the hospital, work closely with families who are experiencing loss, help with funeral planning, organize post-funeral meals, and offer a bereavement support group. Try to get that from a self-help book!

Along with this support comes accountability, and this is where some people balk. To be challenged to adhere to certain religious standards is a tough — but important — dimension of spiritual growth, and I would argue that achieving moral clarity requires the existence of a community every bit as much as practicing Christian charity. Some of my biggest challenges in ministry have arisen out of situations in which I have had to confront church members about thoughtless or selfish acts, such as an older member berating a new member of the church. Many respond with anger and defensiveness, and then show resentment toward me that can last for years.

I hate these conflicts, and yet I believe that ministry includes this sort of guidance. Books, television shows, and the internet simply cannot provide it. *Touched By An Angel* and *Seventh Heaven* are entertaining television fare, but they don't push people to move beyond their comfortable lifestyles. Frankly, in a spiritual marketplace that offers resources ranging from New Age guidebooks to religious classics, a person can find support for any perspective or any passion that feels good. "One thing is for sure," says Denise Giacomozzi May, chaplain for United College Ministries in Northern Virginia, "with so much specialized literature, and so many chat rooms, radio, and television options, our culture is Balkanized, fractured into untold numbers of interest groups and sub-groups that we can very easily — I would say too easily — lose ourselves in a tiny world of like-thinkers or like-believers."

It may seem odd for a pastor to worry about like-thinkers and like-believers, since the church is often accused of enforcing rigid orthodoxy. But I'm concerned when faith comes to be seen as only an individual, private matter. There's no limit to the narcissism of a spirituality that is completely cut off from scripture, tradition, and a community of faith. We are naturally going to become self-centered unless we are challenged to look outward by a congregation that is following the ancient examples of Abraham and Moses.

Not that modern media are inherently lacking. "Something like twenty percent of all Americans use the internet for spiritual purposes," says Steve Waldman, editor-in-chief of beliefnet.com, a website that is designed to appeal to all faiths. I have occasionally turned to this site when I am preparing sermons. "Yes, it is a more personal, private, and in some way intimate form of spirituality. But it is not without depth. These are real relationships that form on our message boards — real consolation is offered, real compassion expressed, real prayers traded."

In fact, the institutional church has hurt itself by failing to use the web to energize its own communities. Churches "still represent the 'trusted brands,' " notes Waldman. "All they have to do is wake up and be creative about the web." Fairfax's McKee believes that the church must be "open to all, seven days a week, 24 hours a day. We must provide an ear to listen; we must provide opportunities to learn about God and about becoming self aware; and we must provide an example." To do this, it is crucial that we take advantage of the internet and other fresh forms of communication to proclaim both obligation and liberation. Fairfax's website now contains information about worship services and mission activities, links to reach pastors, and material for reflection such as prayers and the texts of Sunday sermons.

There's no doubt in my mind that congregational leaders and members still have something special to offer: a community of support and accountability, as well as what Waldman describes as "the feeling of someone holding your hand during a prayer, the emotional charge of a great sermon, the inspiration of gorgeous spiritual music, the evocative smell of incense." But the fact is that our customers are voting with their feet. In a world of spiritual self-help, the church has to find new ways to sell itself as an organization that is accessible, responsive, and relevant to members of an ever more individualistic world.

This raises, for me, the issue of "marketing" — a word that is anathema to many committed Christians. Consider the difficulty I encountered at Calvary Presbyterian when a young man came into my office for a session of premarital counseling and asked me, "Why do you call it Calvary? Did someone in this church fight the Indians?"

For a moment I was puzzled — Indians? — then I realized what he was asking. "It's Calvary," I said, "not cavalry! Calvary is the hill where Jesus died on the cross." He smiled and nodded.

At that point, I knew that Calvary had a marketing problem. Why would anyone come to us for spiritual nourishment if our name evoked Wild West conflict between the Indians and the U.S.

Army Cavalry? And it struck me that if "Calvary" was confusing, "Presbyterian" was downright mystifying, even to people who have always belonged to the denomination. It takes a little knowledge of Greek to understand that "presbyter" means "elder," so a Presbyterian Church is a congregation ruled by elders. We have a fine tradition of decision making by democratically elected elders, but the word "Presbyterian" on a signboard does little to explain our distinctive Christian style to the world.

In short, Calvary Presbyterian Church is not a user-friendly name for a congregation, and this puts the church at a distinct disadvantage in today's Christian marketplace. Many people, especially adults born after 1945, shop for the church that is most convenient, comfortable, and satisfying for them. These shoppers have little denominational loyalty or sense of obligation to any particular community of faith. Instead, they are drawn to churches that have plenty of parking, attractive facilities, and programs that promise to meet their spiritual needs. Researchers such as Dean Hoge of Catholic University have found that many baby boomers are looking for "high-quality Sunday school and youth programs, uplifting worship experiences, and meaningful, authentic small-group experiences." They are looking for liberation from traditional forms, and are searching for a church that will provide them with a promised land of spiritual satisfaction.

Addressing these concerns is a new challenge for most churches, because for years congregations did not have to think about marketing. Their members came to worship out of a sense of duty — religious obligation, you might say — and congregational leaders could count on regular attendance and financial support. Older adults still feel this sense of obligation, and thus are the backbone of many congregations. They continue to support the churches they built or inherited, and they stay in the denominations they have been part of for all or most of their lives.

Today, however, congregations are required to market themselves, because younger adults come to worship only if it feels right. "Boomers see churches as selling a product which they are free to buy or not to buy as they wish," says Hoge, "and they feel perfectly free to change from one supplier to another if there is reason to do so." Even Roman Catholics are now crossing parish boundaries in their search for a church that has a good school, an agreeable priest, meaningful messages, and quality music.

Into this economy have stepped such full-service churches as the Christian Center of Alexandria. This nondenominational congregation offers contemporary praise and worship, drama, and special ministries for singles, children, and youth. As a seven-day-a-week church, its activities go far beyond Sunday worship: There are Saturday prayer groups and Wednesday evening classes, as well as a weekday Christian school and opportunities for mission trips. The church even offers country and western dance lessons!

The Christian Center is much more marketable than Calvary in other ways, too. The builders of Calvary all walked to worship, so the church has no off-street parking; the Christian Center has a huge lot. Calvary has a lovely but inflexible Old English sanctuary with rows of oak pews; the Center has a school gym that functions as its sanctuary and can be modified to accommodate a variety of seating arrangements and worship styles. Calvary was built over fifty years ago, and is beginning to show its age; the Christian Center is about twenty years old and still looks very new and modern. The name "Calvary Presbyterian" is not only mystifying, but it makes some think of difficult doctrines such as predestination; the name "Christian Center" is straightforward and attractive, as is their inviting slogan "People caring for people." In short, Calvary projects the kind of purity and exclusiveness we tend to associate with the covenant, while the Christian Center broadcasts an exodus-style diversity and inclusiveness.

My point is not that congregations such as the Christian Center are superior to traditional, denominational churches. Calvary has a proud history of quality worship and strong community involvement, and for a time grew rapidly through the incorporation of African immigrants. Rather, my point is that contemporary churches like the Christian Center are doing a better job of positioning themselves to attract young and middle-aged Americans who are questing for personal fulfillment and feel little or no institutional loyalty.

119

In the 1990s, three Calvary couples in their twenties and thirties left Alexandria and purchased homes in more distant suburbs; this was a fairly typical migration pattern. They were all faithful, gifted people, and I would have loved for them all to remain in our denomination, but there was no guarantee that this would happen. Blake and Missy, the parents of a disabled child, found a Methodist Church with a special ministry to families in their situation. Peter and Laurel, who served as elders at Calvary, looked for a place that felt like Calvary, visited churches of several denominations, and then settled on a Presbyterian Church. Bette Jo and Kris, both lifelong Presbyterians, joined a large Methodist Church near their new home, one with a variety of programs that enabled them to put their talents, such as Kris' artistic abilities, to use. Four out of six left the Presbyterian denomination, but not because they disliked it; they simply failed to find another Presbyterian Church that met their needs and challenged them to live out their faith.

Church shopping and church hopping are not limited to young laypeople — these trends are seen among future clergy, as well. In the late 1990s, Charles Foster of the Candler School of Theology at Emory University in Atlanta asked his 39 seminarians how many had been members of more than one denomination's congregation. More than two-thirds had. He concludes that "younger adults tend to have higher loyalty to the congregation to which they currently belong than to any denomination." Denominational ties are bound to get even weaker if both lay people and seminarians feel free to hop and shop. This is bad, because denominations are the church groups that support worldwide missions; the training of church clergy; and the taking of stands for peace, justice, and religious freedom on the national and international levels. Individual congregations are not equipped to do this. And theologically, there is a loss of historically based understanding of the faith, as well as unity within the church. The liberation of Moses is edging out the obligations of Abraham, with some rather troubling implications.

So how can traditional congregations such as Calvary and Fairfax Presbyterian carve out a niche in the church market? Not by trying to be more self-consciously Presbyterian, but by focusing on the unique strengths they have as individual congregations.

For a time, Calvary proclaimed itself to be an "International Community Church," and attracted not only large numbers of African immigrants, but also young Americans looking for a multicultural Christian community. Fairfax has a vibrant youth program with a strong emphasis on summer mission projects, and this has been attractive both to young people (there are currently over 100 in the program) and to their parents.

Church leaders also need to realize that many churchgoers expect that worship will be entertaining. This troubles me, because worship is meant to be an opportunity to glorify God and encounter Christ in Word and Sacrament, not a musical concert or self-improvement seminar, but I cannot deny that many young adults are attracted to churches with contemporary praise songs, backed by synthesizers, drums, and electric guitars. At Fairfax, we now have a Jubilee service with contemporary music, in addition to our traditional worship with organ and piano music (a style that is most meaningful to older adults). In my preaching, I try to focus more on scripture than psychology, but I know that people are coming to hear a message of hope and new life, not a lecture on the Bible. In my sermon planning, I have to keep in mind that many attend worship with needs for personal support and reassurance, as well as inspiration and spiritual guidance. There is no getting around the fact that potential new members are looking for uplifting worship services, high-quality Sunday school and youth programs, and meaningful small-group experiences — features of church life that we have to provide, if we want our congregations to grow.

Can traditional churches become more user-friendly without selling out to our individualistic, consumer-focused society? Perhaps. There is certainly nothing wrong with convenient parking, attractive buildings, and music with a contemporary beat. We can make an effort to pull people away from their individualism by gathering the church community around important mission projects such as soup kitchens and tutoring programs. We can even use the web to energize congregational life by providing sites that allow the church to be open to all, seven days a week.

But as we attend to these practical matters, we have to be careful. If traditional preachers lose their prophetic edge, and focus on comfort to the exclusion of challenge, then the church will become nothing more than another self-help group. People should certainly have their legitimate needs met, but they should also be challenged to confess their sins, be reconciled to one another, listen for God's Word, and then do good work in the world. Jesus did not ask people to choose him and use him; instead he called men and women to follow him in a ministry of service to a troubled world.

Maybe such an approach, based on a balancing act between moral clarity and Christian charity, is the commodity that people are really looking for as they shop and hop from church to church. The challenge for congregations — whether traditional or contemporary — is to practice both clarity and charity, so that people will see that these desirable qualities are most readily available in a community of faith, rather than in the self-help section of the local bookstore.

Chapter Eleven

Obligation And Liberation
In A Time Of War

When the airline and hospitality industries were hammered by September 11 and its aftermath, business in churches began to boom. The Friday after the terrorist attacks, my noontime prayer service at Fairfax Presbyterian swelled from the usual half-dozen participants to more than 100. Worship attendance that Sunday was up by 63 percent, from 286 to 466 — more like a High Holy Day than a September Sunday. And participation in services was fifteen percent higher than normal through the end of November. Fellow pastors told me they were seeing much the same pattern within their congregations: In response to an attack on our country that was perpetrated partly in the name of religion, people were turning to religion in droves.

Although the attendance spike that followed September 11 has now disappeared, the impact of the terrorist attacks continues to be felt. Worshipers are coming to Fairfax Presbyterian in search of hope and assurance and a supportive community as they struggle with what it means to live with constant tension. But they are also coming with more complex concerns: Many are seeking solace in a faith that preaches forgiveness, for example, while expressing their conviction of the need for a punitive military response. Members of my congregation are talking more openly about their faith, asking questions about justice, the morality of violence, and the role of the church in responding to conflict.

So, while I take no pleasure in terrorist attacks or anthrax scares or war in the Middle East, in a sense it has been a good time to be the church. Larry Bowen, a professor at George Mason University and a church member for 27 years, told me in November 2001 that the church had helped him live with the conflict between "fear of terrorism" and "business as usual." I think that is partly because the qualities that we all need in order to get through this period of uncertainty — steadfastness, patience, and faithfulness — are better articulated and demonstrated by religious leaders than by most politicians. Abraham and Moses can help us to keep the faith in a time of terrorism and war ... but in some surprising ways.

Certainly the church is offering a solid sense of community to people who are now keenly aware of their need for it. Few are feeling today's stress as acutely as airline employees. "The carefree attitude and ability to 'chum' with the passengers and cockpit crew members has diminished greatly," Karen Williams, a church member and United Airlines flight attendant, told me. With this charged atmosphere exacerbated by the threat of layoffs, she says she has found real comfort in her connection to the church. "I ushered one Sunday and stood there looking at all the people sitting in the congregation. In my mind, I wondered who I could move in with, should I lose my job and my home." The fellow congregants seemed to her like extended family. "It was a reassuring thought," she added.

But beyond the comfort of community and shared values come more challenging questions — about God's role, for example, in recent events. Some national Christian commentators concerned with providing moral clarity have linked terrorism to divine judgment (Jerry Falwell, who later retracted the statement, and Pat Robertson) or to a call to repentance (Charles Colson). Some nonbelievers have cited the attacks as simply the latest example of evil being carried out in the name of religion. I don't agree with any of these views, not because I don't believe in the importance of judgment or repentance in religious life — and not because I'm blind to the potential for people to deliberately misconstrue religious messages.

My problem with the commentators' speculation is that to find God's fingerprints on the events of September 11 is to follow the reasoning of Osama bin Laden, who called the attacks "a punishment from Allah," saying the United States had invited Allah's wrath. While we are certainly flawed individuals in an imperfect country, I cannot believe that God would choose to punish a nation by allowing the slaughter of several thousand office workers. Yes, early biblical accounts do describe a vengeful God and a warrior God, but the Bible contains an evolving understanding of holiness, through both testaments, and eventually reveals a loving God — a Lord of charity — who is willing to perform great acts of sacrifice. To see God as a killer is to be stuck in a religious time warp.

My church members aren't buying the hand-of-God arguments, either. "I do not believe that the attacks were in any way *of God*," reflects Rob McLallen, a money manager and church elder. The bottom line for him is that there is good and evil in the world, and what happened on September 11 "was clearly the result of the presence of evil."

So, much of what my parishioners and I are doing now is trying to find a context for dealing with — and responding to — evil. One member who works for one of the intelligence services says he has "a strong, personal need" to lean on his religious faith while helping our government fight terrorism. "The Islamic fundamentalists who started this war have declared it a holy war and point to their religious beliefs to explain everything they do," he said. "Our government, always extremely cautious to separate church from state, is not well-equipped to understand or deal with this dimension of the war." But, he says, by looking at the religious aspects of this conflict, he is better able to understand why our government's appeals to reason and logic "fall on deaf ears with people who are completely wrapped up in a mystical-messianic worldview where they believe that God will create miracles to overcome all obstacles." He's right: You can find statements in every religious text that, taken alone, could be used to justify any kind of action. It is by exchanging ideas and challenging each other within the community of the church that we can try to make sense of those statements and learn to apply our interpretations to real life.

Exploring the morality of warfare has been the biggest of these challenges for me — and the area in which my own thinking has changed the most as I try to guide my congregation. Until September 11, I would have described myself as a pacifist, someone who embraced the obligation of peacemaking with Abrahamic certainty. I grew up inspired by the nonviolent teachings and strategies of

Mahatma Gandhi and Martin Luther King, Jr., and my preaching consistently opposed the use of violence. That is, until I learned about the passengers who downed the hijacked airplane in Pennsylvania.

Although I have always tried to encourage others to follow Jesus' command to "resist not evil" (Matthew 5:39), in this case resistance appeared to be the highest moral course. I see no virtue in allowing countless others to die — as they surely would have if United Flight 93 had continued under the hijackers' control — because of personal scruples about the use of violence. The passengers on this plane used force to overcome the terrorists, and in so doing were performing the work of liberation favored by followers of Moses. The example of Flight 93 is, to me, the biggest challenge to pure pacifism in modern times — the biggest hurdle for those who want to assert nonviolence as an Abrahamic obligation.

So, if resisting evil makes sense on a hijacked airplane, where else can it be justified? At Fairfax, we've all been wrestling with that issue. Church elder, Jane Carlson, who manages a computer department in an Arlington nonprofit, tells me, "Use of force is the lesser of two evils. When you've got no good choices, you use the least offensive choice. You've got to live with a bad choice." My parishioner, Mike Nelson, a career Air Force officer, fighter pilot, and combat veteran of Vietnam, believes that violence can certainly be moral. Defense of family, society, self, and the right to worship all warrant violence, in his opinion, if that is the only course of action that will prevent defeat. "It has to be a last course," he explains, "but that does not mean it has to be chronologically last. I am perfectly comfortable exercising violence preemptively if reasonable judgment would conclude that inaction will result in outcomes I cannot accept."

In an effort to bring greater clarity to my own thinking as the United States engages in war, I've been asking colleagues how they believe such notions fit within their understanding of theology. A divinity school classmate, John Lentz, who is now a pastor in Cleveland Heights, Ohio, persuaded me that "violence is always an immoral act." John argues, though, that there may be times when immorality requires an immoral response. That reminded me of what

Martin Luther wrote 480 years ago: "Be a sinner and sin boldly, but believe and rejoice in Christ even more boldly, for he is victorious over sin, death, and the world." A realist, Luther believed that every one of us is destined to sin, no matter how hard we try to avoid it. At times, it appears that we need to set aside the fine points of covenant and throw ourselves into the dirty work of exodus.

I've begun articulating the notion that a faithful response to terrorism is to sin boldly, never forgetting that violence is sinful, and that true righteousness lies beyond the realm of human effort: No matter how many bombs we drop or bullets we fire, international harmony is not going to be realized by military action. War cannot, by itself, create a lasting peace, but at the same time it needs to be said that in an imperfect world, resisting evil through violence may sometimes be a necessary evil.

What are the limits to this "sin boldly" approach to war and peace? Clearly, once the pacifism of Jesus is modified by a willingness to restrain evil by warfare, a number of issues arise around allegiance to God and country, and the question of whether Christians can support a particular war. Within a year of September 11, the United States was preparing for an invasion of Iraq, based on suspected links between Saddam Hussein and terrorist activity, but this rush to war led to fierce debate in the church, community, country, and world.

On one level, the invasion of Iraq caused a crisis of allegiance — and even identity — among people who felt torn between loyalty to the United States and loyalty to worldwide Christianity. The contrast between President Bush, who worked hard to drum up support for war, and Christian leaders from around the globe, who took strong stands against it, was quite stark — and all the more difficult to sort out given that Bush spoke often of the importance of faith. After September 11, many Christians, including myself, felt that the use of force against Afghanistan could be morally justified, but fewer supported preemptive war against Iraq.

"As Christians, we try to hold citizenship in two places — the USA and the kingdom of God," observed William H. Willimon, the dean of the chapel at Duke University, in September 2002. "That causes, in the present moment, some tension."

127

It was hard for me to chart a straight course for myself and my parishioners when respected religious leaders were recommending an approach that was so different from the president's. The American Roman Catholic bishops told Bush they could not justify extending the war on terrorism to Iraq unless Saddam Hussein's regime could be linked to the attacks of September 11. One hundred Christian ethicists from more than fifty schools signed a petition saying that the president had failed to make a compelling moral case for a preemptive war. In September 2002, my regional church body, National Capital Presbytery, passed a resolution opposing military action against Iraq at that time. At a World Council of Churches central committee meeting, 37 church leaders signed a statement urging restraint, and the general secretary of the Middle East Council of Churches, Riad Jarjour, Pope John Paul II, and Archbishop of Canterbury-designate Rowan Williams all spoke against resorting to war.

For a worldwide Christian Church that rarely agrees about anything, this was quite a consensus. The widespread religious opposition to invasion put members of my parish in a tough spot, especially military officers, who are accountable to the chain of command and ultimately to the commander-in-chief. In fact, this was an uncomfortable subject for all federal employees, since they have taken an oath of loyalty to the Constitution, and this challenged them to find a way to remain loyal to it while disagreeing with government officials.

Charles Parrott discovered one path through the maze. A USDA administrator and member of Fairfax Presbyterian, he said that since America was founded to be a government "of the people," the suggestion that we must follow the president's lead in order to be a good American is "mere folly." To support the Constitution is, he said, quite different from supporting particular elected officials. As a Christian, Parrott said, he could not endorse an invasion of Iraq. "Although Saddam is reprehensible," he argued, "[since] when does America have the right to attack another country simply because we don't like their leader?"

My parishioner, Esther Elstun, a professor at George Mason University who specializes in twentieth-century German literature, history, and culture, knows all too well from studying Nazi Germany the terrible dilemma that arises when Christian values conflict with the political policies and objectives of a person's homeland. Although she found no conflict between her Christian convictions and our country's principles as expressed in the Constitution and the Bill of Rights, she said that Iraq may pose a conflict of allegiance, for she is convinced that an invasion "cannot by any stretch of the imagination be reconciled with the teachings of Jesus." She considered such an action to be both un-Christian and un-American, "which I suspect is why the proponents of the proposed attack prefer to use such contemptible euphemisms as 'preemptive strike' and 'regime change.' " Elstun took a very Abrahamic position on this conflict, basing her opposition on a strong sense of obligation toward the teachings of Jesus.

Of course, some Christians took a very different stand regarding an invasion of Iraq. "I believe that God expects us to help people who are oppressed," said John Warburton, a church member who spent a career in the Air Force. Referring to Sunday-service scripture lessons that covered the flight of the Israelites from Egypt, he pointed out that God allowed many Egyptians to be killed at the hand of Moses. "Why?" he asked me. "I think it is because the Egyptian rulers were somewhat like the leadership in Iraq. Their people are oppressed." My parishioner, Tim Tarzier, a retired U.S. Air Force officer born in formerly communist Latvia, added that although he does have moral problems with a conflict involving loss of life, he believes that "neutralizing a known and demonstrated threat is a way to avoid a greater conflict."

Here we see that, in the case of war, there is a reversal of the expected obligation-liberation dichotomy. The liberals are focusing on covenant, on an obligation to follow the clear nonviolent teachings of Jesus, while the conservatives are basing their position on exodus, on their desire to do the work of liberation on behalf of the oppressed people of Iraq. While liberals are normally attuned to exodus and conservatives to covenant, the war in Iraq turned this pattern on its head. Abraham and Moses are clearly fluid role models, not always linked to conservative and liberal political categories.

For President Bush to gain the full support of the American Christian community, he had to make a case for invasion that reached across this wide religious spectrum. To do so, he spoke often about the liberation of the Iraqi people, and used the words of a hymn, "There's Power In The Blood," as part of his 2003 State of the Union speech. He spoke of the "power, wonder-working power" of "the goodness and idealism and faith of the American people" — failing to note, however, that the "wonder-working power" in the hymn refers to the blood of the Lamb of God, Jesus Christ. My colleague, Fritz Ritsch, pastor of Bethesda Presbyterian Church, found this unspoken but apparently deliberate parallel between Americans and Jesus to be "disturbing, to say the least." Clearly, we are not as generous as Jesus, nor as innocent and vulnerable as the Lamb of God, but for Bush these connections helped build a religious justification for confronting the "evil" before us. Writing in *The Washington Post* on March 2, 2003, Ritsch observed that the most striking characteristic of Bush's use of religion "is its relentless triumphalism." Bush is not so much an Abraham or a Moses as he is a David — a warrior who wants to pull together a secular vision and a set of spiritual aspirations.

Traditionally, born-again Christians, such as the president, have been more concerned about personal morality, such as sex and drinking, than about community morality, as expressed in positions on Christian pacifism and just-war doctrine. In the case of war with Iraq, Bush's very personal commitment to fighting evil may have prevented him from hearing the nuanced ethical discussions going on in the larger Christian community. There was not much talk coming out of the White House about whether the invasion of Iraq met classic just-war criteria: War that is waged by proper authority, for a just cause, with right intent, and using proper means.

Not that the president has ever been reluctant to jump into the tricky work of defining God's involvement in American life. "We cannot know all that lies ahead," he said in his September 11 anniversary speech in 2002. "Yet we do know that God has placed us together in this moment, to grieve together, to stand together, to serve each other, and our country." There is certainly truth in these words, but they should not lead us to believe that all Christians will support any and all American military actions — especially given our religious commitment to warfare that leans toward self-defense and protection of noncombatants, and away from aggression and first strikes. In 2002, William Willimon told me that he was trying to pay more attention to the Middle East Council of Churches than to the president, and said, "I feel closer to Christians who are there — and there are a number of fellow Christians in Iraq — than to the generals who are here."

My colleague, Roy W. Howard, pastor of St. Mark Presbyterian Church in Rockville, Maryland, felt this tension keenly, and he called together a group of about twenty church leaders in the fall of 2002 to discuss the threat of war as both a theological and pastoral matter. While admitting that "my pledge of allegiance to the United States is in constant creative tension with my pledge of allegiance to God," he explained that he didn't support an invasion of Iraq at the time, since he was not convinced that all efforts to disarm the Iraqi regime had been exhausted. Nor did he believe that attacking Iraq at that time would necessarily accomplish the goal of a more just and peaceful world.

But the day may come, Howard admitted, "as it came for Christians resisting Hitler, that an attack on Saddam Hussein is the absolute only way to prevent the loss of millions of lives." He admired the German Christians, members of the Resistance, who attempted to assassinate Hitler, but he recalled that they did it in a contrite spirit, "casting themselves upon the mercy of God and repenting of their sin." We were not at that point, he believed, since one of the criteria of the centuries-old Christian doctrine of just war is that all other possibilities for peace have been exhausted. He felt that there was still much that could be done internationally to bring about Iraqi compliance with all U.N. resolutions and to move vigorously to eliminate all weapons of mass destruction. Howard argued that "Christians can work with Iraqi citizens to demonstrate visibly against the actions of their leaders which lead to human rights violations, death, and destruction of their people." This thoughtful approach to the issue could have been part of a blueprint for Bush, one that would not have required immediate military action.

The president needed to address these misgivings, using both political and theological language, if he was going to win the support of Christian leaders at home and abroad. As it turned out, he didn't, and one of the bishops of his own denomination, the United Methodist Church, went on television to criticize the Bush administration's war rhetoric. Going to war with Iraq "violates God's law and the teachings of Jesus Christ," said the bishop, sounding more like an obligation-keeper than a liberation-seeker.

The tension between liberal concern for religious obligation and conservative commitment to forceful liberation continued during the run-up to war with Iraq in the spring of 2003 and beyond, as Americans clashed with Iraqi forces and then tried to restore order to the country. I found myself shepherding a more divided congregation than usual, with some of my parishioners saying that our troops were performing the godly work of liberation, using their weapons to free the oppressed, while others argued that Jesus would take a stand against the war and armed occupation, since he opposed the use of violence. I couldn't help but notice that there was ample theological support for either view, however, I tended to oppose the intervention and urge restraint.

Through it all, I preached Sunday sermons, knowing that I was in a powerful position, standing before a crowd of worshipers, armed with conviction and the scriptures of my choosing. Yet, while I called for restraint and diplomacy, I saw danger in using theology to justify personal political convictions, so I resisted the temptation to preach one-sided sermons that would confirm the views of some parishioners and infuriate others. I tried to keep Abraham and Moses in a kind of creative tension, so that followers of both role models would see the contributions that each character can make.

Not that we ministers are supposed to focus on pleasing our people by keeping everything in perfect balance. I risked alienating some members with criticism of the war, reminding them, for example, that the Lord abhors our worship of the false gods of western affluence, worldly power, and high technology. I agree with Michael J. Easley, the senior pastor-teacher of Immanuel Bible Church in Springfield, Virginia, when he says, "I think my 'job' is to clearly teach the scriptures, not be persuaded by what may or may not be our people's views." But that statement raises the question, "Which passage of scripture?"

The Bible offers both the story of God's liberation of the Israelites from oppression in Egypt and Jesus' command to turn the other cheek. I could have built a pro- or anti-war case depending on whether I preached on a story of the Israelites destroying their enemies by the edge of the sword (Joshua 6:21) or on Jesus commanding his disciple to "Put your sword back into its place; for all who take the sword will perish by the sword" (Matthew 26:52). I've come to realize that it is a mistake to use scriptural stories in such isolation. The genius of religious leaders like Martin Luther King, Jr., and Desmond Tutu is that their messages come not from individual passages but from basic biblical concepts, such as love of one's enemies, which they have used to transform the thinking of vast segments of society.

"There are three ways to use scripture in preaching — text, context, and pretext," says Rabbi Jack Moline of Agudas Achim Congregation in Alexandria, Virginia. All are legitimate, he argues, but "to be truly faithful and honest, the religious leader should own up to which process is at play. I find it helpful to acknowledge my prejudices before I begin pontificating," he tells me. He makes a point that I try to follow, but I can't pretend that I can entirely separate my political views from my interpretation of the scriptures.

I've become aware, once again, that a political gap often exists between clergy and parishioners. I am more liberal than my parishioners in many areas, such as in my desire for more diversity in the life of the church. Such a difference can be enlightening, as one of my church members, Thomas Larsen, a retired Air Force officer, discovered when he arrived several decades ago at Fairfax Presbyterian with a conservative point of view. "Our senior pastor, Henry Baumann, was very liberal," he recalls, even participating in the Civil Rights marches in the 1960s, but he "gave such excellent sermons that I always came away feeling that I had learned something, and that we had grown closer in our political/social/theological thinking."

Congregations often fracture, though, and lose their effectiveness as a force for good in the community, when clergy become radical or dogmatic. Liberal "extremism," says Methodist pastor Bob Kaylor, my colleague at the *Homiletics* preaching journal, "makes for a 'one note' preacher. Those who pick up a particular social issue and constantly bang away at it seem to alienate at least half the people they're addressing." At the other end of the spectrum, Kaylor says, are those "whose theology is so rigidly dogmatic that it smacks of legalism and exclusion."

Whether they follow Abraham or Moses, extremists of all persuasions are probably preaching to the choir, picking up on political trends rather than creating them. The danger of religious extremists is that they are willing to choose one scriptural passage and use it not to challenge people, but to fire up those who are already prone to follow the preacher's line of thought. Because preachers have used the Bible to support and justify all types of horrors and injustices — slavery, anti-Semitism, the subordination of women, to name a few — it is critically important that pastors and parishioners wrestle with scripture together. This tragic history makes Michelle Fincher, a member of my church, both nervous and cautious about what she hears from the pulpit. "Regardless of how much I respect and admire the preacher," she tells me, "I am responsible for studying and asking questions — of the government, of the church, and of myself — in order to develop an informed, prayerful opinion or decision on ethical issues."

If we clergy can create communities in which controversial issues are discussed openly and respectfully, then we'll stand a chance of identifying dangerous political positions or flawed scriptural interpretations and of influencing people more than we can — or should — with our Sunday morning monologues. Bruce Douglass, a faculty member at Georgetown University and an elder at Lewinsville Presbyterian Church in McLean, Virginia, believes that in this time of shrill rhetoric, "it may well be that one of the most valuable services the churches can perform is simply to provide a setting where people with differing opinions can come together to exchange opinions in an atmosphere of mutual respect." Out of such dialogues, the church may decide to act — as Henry

Baumann and members of Fairfax Presbyterian did in the '60s, when they felt inspired to step out and work for Civil Rights.

All of this sometimes makes me wonder how I should seek — or hope — to influence my congregation. I want to challenge people morally and spiritually, but I am aware that their outlooks are often deeply entrenched. I constantly check my own motivation: Have I questioned the invasion of Iraq because Jesus said, "Put your sword back into its place," or have I used this passage to justify my own political opposition to a preemptive strike? That process of questioning has made me realize that while I would gladly join a demonstration of solidarity with Iraqi Christians — a statement I believe to be religiously grounded — I would feel deeply uneasy in a protest against administration policies.

If we fail to wrestle with these issues, personally and congregationally, then we can easily remain trapped in our preconceived notions. If, on the other hand, we pastors and church members keep dialogue alive, and perform an ongoing balancing act with competing biblical and theological positions, then we will stand a chance of discovering an unconventional truth together. One very practical contribution that our churches can make is to provide a place — within a community of shared values and mutual concern — where people can explore the morality of warfare, and have discussion and dialogue about pacifism and just-war criteria. The community of faith remains the very best place to debate the relative merits of obligation and liberation, clarity and charity, purity and diversity, covenant and exodus, as well to listen carefully to the competing claims of our ancient role models Abraham and Moses.

Epilogue

Fairfax Presbyterian Church devoted about a year, from July 2003 through September 2004, to an observance of its fiftieth anniversary. Such celebrations always involve considering how life has altered over time, and looking at this church, I was struck by the wrenching changes it has undergone — along with most other mainline Protestant congregations.

Once it was a booming, traditional, middle-of-the-road church that served as a meeting ground for a large, diverse community of believers who may not have agreed on politics or shared the same cultural outlook, but who identified themselves with a particular religious tradition and proudly wore the label "Presbyterian," with all that it implied. Over the years, however, it has lost members left and right to more specialized, politically focused churches and communities.

In this regard, the story of Fairfax Presbyterian echoes a broader, troubling change in denominations across the nation. It is a change that could lead to the disappearance of churches that strive for balance in religious practice and belief, that seek moderation and a way to combine respect for obligation with an understanding of the need for liberation. This shrinkage of the moderate religious middle reflects the polarization of contemporary politics, where the most powerful voices now speak from the far right and left. In fact, an in-depth poll by the Pew Research Center for the People and the Press revealed that partisan differences over both national security and domestic issues had reached a historic high in the Summer of 2003. The United States "remains a country that is almost evenly divided politically," said the center, "yet further apart than ever in its political values." And, a 2004 poll done by Public Agenda, a nonpartisan research organization, revealed that church-going Americans have grown increasingly intolerant of politicians making compromises on issues such as abortion and gay rights. These trends could indicate "more polarized political thinking,"

137

said Ruth Wooden, president of Public Agenda. "There do not seem to be very many voices arguing for compromise today."

What we've lost in this process of polarization is our belief in the importance of meeting grounds — communities where people of diverse opinions and perspectives may gather, talk, debate, and argue. Church is, in my opinion, the healthiest place for people to wrestle with difficult issues such as presidential politics, church-state relations, immigration, virtue, homosexuality, and war. To me as a minister, given that we live in a world being so profoundly affected by religious extremists of all faiths, this is a loss we cannot afford.

Fairfax Presbyterian grew quickly through the '50s as it rode the wave of the baby boom and responded to postwar interest in religious life. Its early expansion was helped by the fact that it was the only Presbyterian congregation in Fairfax City, making it a logical choice for Fairfax residents with this particular denominational background. By the end of the decade, the church had about 600 members and was becoming known for its progressive educational ministry, offering a racially integrated preschool program and a set of adult classes that certainly sounded ahead of their time: ethics, politics, the Middle East, death, and dying.

Members had different political and theological beliefs, and a variety of views on obligation and liberation, moral clarity, and Christian charity. I've been told that at least one person left Fairfax Presbyterian when the pastor followed the call of Moses and became active in the Civil Rights Movement, but for the most part, members came together around a shared denominational identity.

Back then, whether you were Presbyterian or Lutheran or Baptist, you tended to choose a denomination that either you or your spouse had known since childhood. But today, we are witnessing a deterioration of denominational loyalty, and Protestant Christians now think of themselves, as so much of society seems to, in more political terms — as conservatives or liberals, instead of members of a particular religious tradition. Sociologists say that people look for residential communities where they can be surrounded by those who share their political views and cultural proclivities. Now, it seems they are also gravitating toward specialized communities of faith that are at opposite ends of the theological spectrum: on the right, conservative churches that preach traditional theology and morality in a covenant-keeping style, and on the left, liberal, inclusive congregations that offer a range of theological perspectives and sexual orientations in response to the exodus message. In 1988, sociologist, Robert Wuthnow, was one of the first to observe that denominationalism is eroding and that new coalitions are forming across denominations — coalitions focused on abortion, biblical inerrancy, sexual issues, and other shared concerns. The result is that congregations are becoming groups of like-minded individuals, instead of cross sections of the religious community.

A former member of my congregation, Ellen Will, grew up as the daughter of a Presbyterian minister in a Rhode Island town that was more than ninety percent Roman Catholic. As a member of a minority denomination, it was important for her to gather each Sunday with fellow Presbyterians, but when she and her family began to attend Fairfax Presbyterian in the '90s, she says that what she encountered was "fuzzy" teaching about Christianity and evolution — she was shocked that a church school teacher described the creation story in Genesis as "strictly an allegory."

She and her family were also troubled by a skit featuring a man dressed as a woman, playing a God-like character named "Godmother Grace." The point of the play was that God is really spirit, neither male nor female, but her sons simply found it "weird." In both cases, Ellen and her family witnessed attempts by the Presbyterian Church to combine new concepts with ancient traditions — but it didn't work for them.

The Wills ended up worshiping at the more conservative, non-denominational Immanuel Bible Church in Springfield, Virginia, which felt like a good fit in terms of biblical teaching. Ellen tells me she has a number of friends who have also departed the denominations they were raised in, feeling that their churches had become too liberal. Two of them left Methodist Churches, one couple because the new minister brought his live-in girlfriend to join him in the parsonage, and the other because of the issue of homosexual ordination. This latter issue is not just a congregational concern, of course. In 2003, Anglican world leaders gathered in England to try to avert a split in their church after the election of a gay bishop in New Hampshire.

Ellen believes that it's more common for conservative, evangelical believers to leave mainline denominations and go to conservative "Bible" churches, but on a smaller scale, an exodus is occurring on the left as well. The highly inclusive Unitarian Universalist denomination is growing at a rate of one percent a year, mainly through transfers, with almost ninety percent of new UU members coming from other religions. Linda Olson Peebles, minister of religious education at the Unitarian Universalist Church of Arlington, Virginia, tells me that her denomination sees a wide range of theological orientations, mostly "on the left of center," and that UU congregations are a blend of liberal Christians, religious humanists, atheists, and people who would describe themselves simply as "spiritual." They tend to rally around freedom of belief and trust in human reason.

So people are tending to move to the right toward obligation, or to the left toward liberation. But I have to wonder: What's wrong with the combination of tradition and innovation for which my own church strives? My frustration is that people are abandoning denominations — like my own — that are trying to maintain a creative tension between time-honored truths and new theological insights, between conservative and liberal, if you like, and are trying to stake out a middle ground of moderation and reasonableness that seems so sorely lacking in many parts of society today.

In the Presbyterian Church, we certainly base our beliefs on the Bible, but we also affirm that God is leading us to new understandings about what it means to be good and faithful people in the world today — an approach that requires a certain willingness to change. Although we once understood the Bible to support slavery and the second-class status of women, for example, we now read it and hear God calling for freedom and equality. We are a church that is supposed to be in the process of reforming itself, and this has certainly been my emphasis since becoming pastor of Fairfax in 2001. While I preach biblical sermons, I also stress that we worship a God who is always surprising us — sometimes even through the appearance of "Godmother Grace."

Such an approach challenges people to perform a balancing act, always weighing conservative certainty against liberal openness, obligation against liberation. And this, unfortunately, is a game that fewer and fewer people are willing to play. Loren Mead, an Episcopalian priest and founding president of the Alban Institute in Bethesda, an interfaith organization that works to support congregations, observes that Protestants today seem less able to tolerate differences — they feel pressure to resolve contentious issues such as those involving sex or gender, no matter the cost in relationships. Churches are living in a constant state of conflict, he says, with people on different sides of an issue drifting apart, shutting down dialogue and often using derogatory terms to belittle their opponents. What is killed in these struggles is the notion that church can be a meeting ground for diverse points of view, a place for conversation, discovery, and growth. "When congregations fracture," says Mead, "we lose the chance to learn to deal with differences, to solve conflicts within a community of caring."

Although congregations should be models of reconciliation in an increasingly shattered society, the opposite is often true. My colleague, Roy Howard, pastor of Saint Mark Presbyterian Church in Rockville, Maryland, tells me that some church professionals are actually encouraging polarization, instead of resisting it. "Church growth manuals that have proliferated in the past several years advise that 'like attracts like,' and leaders should be positioning their ministry to attract people who are just like them," he says.

While these churches do seem to be succeeding in attracting members, Howard laments this style of growth, noting that "this kind of church bears no resemblance to the church described in the New Testament of rich and poor, strong and weak." Although dividing into congregations of like-minded people who agree on issues may be easier to live with, it cannot be truly healthy. We grow into deeper understanding by conversation and relationships with people who are different from us, and by exploring the creative tension provided by covenant and exodus.

So, what is the future of church life? Personalized faith and comfort-fit congregational options? Or the abandonment of community life altogether, in what sociologist Alan Wolfe tells me is the danger that "we will lose congregational life of any kind as Americans turn away from institutions in favor of home churching, the internet, or other such innovations"? (Of course, this trend will not go that far, he assures me, since "we remain a church-going people.")

My own fear is that we will continue to lose congregations that strive for balance in an increasingly polarized world, congregations like my own. While it's true that we moderates are often seen as lukewarm, and are accused by some of not being "true believers," I'm convinced that our congregations are important. I am committed to what we are doing in Fairfax, and our approach is clearly attractive to some — our church is growing a little again, reversing a decline that began in 1990 and saw total membership drop from 1,200 to 800. But, the future is far from clear and I am aware that one congregation does not create a denominational trend.

Still, I can only hope that when Fairfax Presbyterian Church celebrates its 100th anniversary in 2054, my children will look back and remember not just the comfort of church, but also the challenge of stimulating classes and conversations in a community of diverse points of view. For me, the richness of our faith is discovered when liberation is given equal weight alongside obligation, and when Christian charity is pursued as passionately as moral clarity. People of faith should be open to innovations such as women in ministry, multicultural worship, the ordination of gays and lesbians, and a new emphasis on mission-minded ministry. At the same time, it is important for them to honor traditional styles of worship and ministry that support moral clarity and enable people to maintain their covenant with God. Most of all, Christians are challenged to be receptive to the surprises that Moses and Abraham will undoubtedly bring their way, such as when the threat of terrorism turns liberals into proponents of religious obligation and conservatives into advocates of forceful liberation.

Openness to surprise — how hard this is for us, whether we line up on the covenant or exodus end of the spectrum. And yet, as people of faith, we are challenged every day to trust God to lead us to a new and better future, and we are called to participate in the shaping of a more faithful, just, and peaceful world. But this willingness to look to the future and help build the promised land is something that is sorely missing in the church today, whether we consider ourselves to be followers of Abraham or Moses, obligation-keepers or liberation-seekers.

A generation ago, American religious leaders were not afraid to step out in faith and work for the transformation of the world. In the '60s, the Protestant theologian, Reinhold Niebuhr, influenced the Kennedy administration, bringing his tough-minded "Christian realism" and anti-communist views to bear on debates over the Berlin crisis and the use of nuclear weapons. The Reverend Martin Luther King, Jr., linked passionate preaching to leadership of the Civil Rights Movement. And Yale chaplain, William Sloane Coffin, Jr., used his university pulpit to oppose the Vietnam War. These men didn't hesitate to bring their faith to bear on public policy, and on what they perceived as society's injustices or government's errors.

Today, religious leaders generally tend to concentrate on private, not public, life. Even Christian activists such as Pat Robertson or James Dobson focus chiefly on the family or on issues, such as abortion or gay marriage, that touch people in the realm of their private lives, rather than talking about using theology to shape a better world. Most of us in church leadership today are pastors, quietly tending to our flocks and their internal needs, rather than prophets, challenging our people to look outward and commit themselves to creating a more just society.

Is it possible, though, for religious leaders to be prophetic without crossing the line into politics? Probably not, and this is where being forward-looking becomes controversial. When Isaiah cried out, "seek justice, rescue the oppressed, defend the orphan, plead for the widow" (Isaiah 1:17), he was making a political statement. But due to the fragmentation of our culture, our churches, and our public policies, "the prophetic voice is quieter today because we don't know what to say," observes my colleague Jay Click, the pastor of Grace Presbyterian Church in Springfield, Virginia. "Many of us decry the growing gap between rich and poor, but there does not seem to be a consensus about how to address that." We pastors are struggling with a disconnect between what the Bible teaches and what constitutes an effective political statement, having discovered that the scriptural mandate to help the poor does not translate easily into federal welfare programs. We don't know which political position will actually succeed in bringing "good news to the poor," release to the captives, and freedom to the oppressed (Luke 4:18-19).

On top of this, many of us in pastoral positions are afraid of stirring up controversy, or causing division. Ken Kern, an activist lawyer and member of a Unitarian Church in Indianapolis, tells me that he tries to bring challenging programs on public issues — the administration's foreign policy or elimination of the estate tax — to his fellow congregants, but "church members seem much more comfortable with issues that do not involve challenging the 'system.' " He believes today's church leaders "are concerned about their jobs so they tend to reflect the composite view of their congregations." For most of us, the key to job security is pastoral care, not prophetic pronouncements.

I worry about this tendency in myself and others, because I believe the role of pastor is incomplete without a prophetic dimension. We ministers sometimes forget that Jesus, our role model, not only cared for hurting individuals, but also shattered the cultural conventions of his day and turned his society upside down. In a new book about her father, Niebuhr's daughter, Elisabeth Sifton, criticizes the big preachers of her father's day, men like Norman Vincent Peale and Billy Graham, describing them as men who "never risked their tremendous personal popularity by broaching a difficult spiritual subject, and rarely lifted a finger to help a social cause." This is a harsh judgment, and I think it needs to be said that there is value in the kind of preaching the Peales and the Grahams of the world do, inspiring people to deepen their relationship with God.

But the Bible is clear about the need to "do justice" (Micah 6:8). This call echoes to me in today's world, and I want to make an effort to avoid being seen as a pious, do-nothing pastor. As I lead my congregation into the next fifty years of ministry and mission at Fairfax Presbyterian Church, I want to keep my people

144

looking forward, and embracing the challenge of working for the transformation of the world — whether they see themselves as obligation-keepers or liberation-seekers.

The key to moving forward, as I see it, is to expand our definition of spiritual growth, which goes beyond the personal and has a societal component as well. We have seen this in various national struggles: with fascism during World War II, with race relations in the Civil Rights Movement, with gender issues in the women's movement, and with communism during the Cold War. Such periods of conflict shaped our understanding of freedom, justice, and equality. They contributed to our spiritual growth, and as such were rightly part of any pastor's prophetic agenda. A minister didn't have to be with Dietrich Bonhoeffer in Nazi Germany or Dorothy Day in the slums of New York to take a bold, socially active stand for the faith.

The issues we face today — welfare reform, immigration, globalization — may prove to be equally significant, and it will be a challenge for religious leaders to use theology to help shape a better society. People like Jesse Jackson or Ron Sider, the founder of Evangelicals for Social Action, an association that promotes Christian involvement in social, cultural, and public policy issues, are making an effort in this area. Although they may be inspired by different visions of exodus and covenant, they are united in their commitment to social action.

But every parish pastor is challenged to translate faith into works, whether by marching in a protest or working quietly for affordable housing. At the covenant end of the spectrum I have found Ralph Weitz, the stewardship pastor of Immanuel Bible Church in Springfield, Virginia. He is deeply concerned about the damage that credit card debt does to individuals, families, and society, so he conducts seminars and workshops to teach people how to avoid this burden. And, at the exodus end is my seminary classmate, John Lentz, the president of NOAH, a faith-based organizing group in Cleveland that has stood up against predatory lending. John and this group have helped people move more than $500,000 to lending institutions that have signed a document declaring they do not engage in this practice.

145

The voices of religious leaders have made an important contribution to past political debates, and their voices are needed today. We pastors have an obligation to speak and act from the perspective of our faith, and do whatever we can to motivate our people to work for the transformation of the world. On a practical level, we can begin by making sure that our churches serve as meeting grounds — places for discussion, dialogue, and constructive debate. We can strive for a balance between traditional truths and new theological insights in our preaching and our teaching. And we can give as much attention to public life as we do to private life, so that the transformation of the world will never be a lower priority than the transformation of individual lives. In the end, if we keep these concerns in proper balance, we'll find that they are all intertwined — there is really no separation between the spiritual growth of our parishioners, the health of our communities of faith, and the creation of a more faithful, just, and peaceful world.

The contemporary Christian conflicts we face do not always have to be battles with winners and losers, you see — the perspectives of Abraham and Moses can help us to discover the future that the Lord desires for all his children. The next fifty years of my congregation, like the next half-century of Christianity in the United States, is not completely clear to me — but I know that it will remain healthy if both covenant and exodus are honored, and if faith is continuously translated into action. God has always used both obligation-keepers and liberation-seekers to advance his holy will, and this is as true today as it has ever been, as we wander together toward the promised land.